# God in the Box

Peter Bell

Onwards and Upwards Publishers
Berkeley House, 11 Nightingale Crescent, Leatherhead,
Surrey, KT24 6PD.
**www.onwardsandupwards.org**

---



Printed in the UK.

ISBN: 978-1-907509-86-5
Typeface: Sabon LT

---

# Endorsements

This book goes to the grass root of Christianity, and Peter is very open about how situations have impacted his life and how the Lord has used these to help his faith grow. It is a must read for all, whatever level of faith they have, because we can learn so much from one another.

**Ian Sadler**
National Relationship Manager, Ansvar Insurance
Trustee, Gateway Christian Church, Eastbourne

I wish I had read this book when I was a young Christian, but I'm glad I have read it now. Peter Bell spells out the adventure of living life to the full as a Christian. Readable. Practical. Inspirational.

**Max Sinclair**
Evangelist and teacher, Treasures in Heaven Trust
Elder

"There's no box large enough to put God in, but still people try."

By skilfully weaving together Scripture, personal experience and down-to-earth teaching, Peter walks you, the reader, through the dynamics of discovering who God really is and how to become the effective Christian God intended you to be.

Wherever you are on your journey, this book will spur you on in the right direction. I heartily recommend it.

**Reverend David Wood**
Pastor, Bromley Common Baptist Church, Bromley

# Acknowledgements

Thanks to Pamela, Sue, Martin, Audrey and Ian for their encouragement to complete this work and for their helpful advice and comments.

**Peter Bell**
**August 2013**

# About the Author

Peter Bell has been working as an insurance broker for forty years. He joined his father's business, A. T. Bell Insurance Brokers Ltd in 1973, which focused on providing insurance services to churches, charities and the not-for-profit community. The company grew and developed, and Peter became managing director and owner. He sold the client portfolio in 2010 to another successful insurance broking business, similarly run on Christian values, Access Insurance, where he continues to work as a broker and director.

He is active in church activities and is a trustee and the administrator of Unity Church, Orpington.

Peter has lived in the South London area all his life. He married Pamela in 1980, and they enjoy being involved in the life of the church and share many of the same interests such as gardening, music, being members of a local concert band, exploring places of beauty and historic houses, cats – and just relaxing with a book.

You can contact Peter by writing to **author.bell@gmail.com**.

# Contents

PREFACE .......... 7

INTRODUCTION. Don't Keep God in a Box .......... 15

1. Guidance – A New Sense of Direction .......... 17

2. God's Amazing Love – Breaks Down Barriers .......... 23

3. What is Faith? .......... 29

4. God, Jesus and the Holy Spirit – How Do They Fit Together? .......... 39

5. Communication is Vital .......... 47

6. Practical and Effective Christian Living .......... 55

7. Our Attitudes, Behaviour and Time Use .......... 69

8. The Armour of God .......... 76

9. What Are You Going to Do Now? .......... 85

APPENDIX. One Hundred Per Cent for God .......... 92

"Teach me to do your will, for you are my God; may your good Spirit lead me on level ground."

Psalm 143:10

# PREFACE

Once I found myself asking, what am I doing with my Christian belief? Am I *really living* as a Christian or do I *merely exist* as a Christian?

I didn't have any Damascus road conversion; mine was gradual, being born into a Christian home. I was taught the way of God by my parents and was encouraged to attend church and Crusaders. I remember saying a prayer one day, when I was about eight, asking Jesus into my life. I continued living what I thought to be a Christian life, gradually learning more from the Bible and my parents, until I had a gospel knowledge based on the facts of the Bible. I thought that I now knew how to live as expected.

Through school, college and then into work, I still thought that I was doing things correctly and that attending church and being a Crusader leader was helping my Christian belief. It was indeed giving me experience in expressing what I knew to others. However, one-to-one witnessing was so very hard – what to say and how to say it – and if it didn't come over correctly, what was I to do then?

I went to some Billy Graham crusades and remember at Spree '73, in Earl's Court arena, recommitting my life to God. I knew then that I needed to do more than just exist with a Christian tag pinned on my chest. After a few years I was back into my nice, complacent situation, secure job, living at home with my parents, content with my friends at church.

In 1980 I was married, and that brought a different routine to life. Just before our wedding I did what I had put off for a long time: I was baptised by full immersion, to show an outward expression of my faith in God.

It was a great and joyful event, publicly declaring to others my belief in God – but how did I really feel? It was special but nothing seemed to change in my Christian life. Now married, I continued to attend church and still had many of the same friends. Gradually I became more involved in church life, joining the youth work leadership in Pathfinders, and later joined the music group. I was still that 'existing' Christian – knowing the truth, teaching others about it, but not really doing anything with it!

The years rolled on and my faith in God didn't change. I knew that I had Jesus in me and with me, but through listening to one or two sermons in 1993 I had to seriously consider where I really was with God and what He wanted to do with my life.

In other words, I had been brought by God to re-examine myself, to look at myself and question my very existence. I had been asking what *I was doing* with God, rather than the real question of what *God wanted to do* with me. I had to change the emphasis away from me somehow possessing God and considering what to do with Him, to the realisation of being possessed by God and giving myself to Him, for Him to do with me as He chose.

My faith had to be real, had to be living, not merely existing. In September 1994, I was challenged to learn more about the reality of the Holy Spirit, which up until then I had had little real experience of, except to know that the Spirit is our comforter and it is the Spirit through whom we have an open channel to Jesus and to God. I spoke to other Christians, including my father-in-law, who had just experienced a renewing sense of God's Spirit, and saw that he was fired up for the Lord. How was this possible? What had he done to change that much?

Being curious I wanted to find out – but how? I went to a meeting at another church where, after the worship, Bible teaching, prayer and praise, the congregation were invited to receive the ministry of the Holy Spirit. This was all new to me; these people had a living faith that you could see and touch – it was amazing.

I was standing in a crowd of people who were being prayed over by the ministry team. A member of the team asked me what I wanted to be prayed for. This was difficult; what does one ask for in that situation?

Then the words just came out of my mouth. I said that I wanted whatever God wanted to give me and that I had an open heart to receive. Prayer was said, and in a matter of minutes my legs couldn't hold me up and I fell backwards onto the floor! It was a feeling of floating; I didn't feel the floor hit me. I was just lying there – for how long I don't know; it doesn't matter.

What I do know is that I felt as though I was enveloped in a warm blanket from my head to my toes. It was, I believe, the beautiful warm presence of God engulfing me; His Holy Spirit filled me completely. I was praying to God, my Saviour, who was so close to me. I could have stayed there soaking up His glory and His love all night.

I found out that night that God's Spirit can touch each of us in a way that, humanly speaking, we could not have dreamt of; it was glorious. From that day I have had a new yearning to read God's word, a yearning to pray and talk to others of His love, and a yearning to talk to God, my maker, as a real friend. My life has a much deeper meaning, I have a new outlook on the world, my faith is much deeper and I have a much greater awareness of God's love. When I dwell on Him and on what He has done for me, it just blows my mind! I am filled with gratitude and I just want to praise and thank Him.

I also became more aware of wanting to pray to God and praise Him on a regular basis, and it was during one of these times that He prompted me about the theme of this book (although it was some time before I started writing). I had never written anything before except for a few short stories for my godchildren.

The question that I asked myself was how I was going to write a meaningful book that people could understand and take action on; a book that would be simple and straightforward and applicable to daily life. What were the contents going to be? I thought, "Great idea, but no, I couldn't do that!" Mistake number one! I had fallen into the "I can't do it" trap. Of course I couldn't do it! But God could and has.

I was reflecting on scripture one morning, reading the account of Peter telling Cornelius the good news of Christ, recorded in Acts chapter 10. I had read this account before and had heard it preached about, but this time it was as if I had come with a fresh mind; it was new to me and its meaning seemed to leap off the page.

Peter, having gone to Cornelius, obeying God and witnessing his conversion, then told the other apostles what had happened and why he had done it.

> **Acts 11:17**
> *So if God gave them the same gift as He gave us, who believed in the Lord Jesus Christ, who was I to think that I could oppose God?*

That verse hit me. Was I opposing God? I thought and prayed about this, and it was shown clearly to me that God not only wanted me to put down my experiences in writing but wanted me to help others to grow in their relationship with Him too. That was a daunting thought as I had no knowledge of how to do this – but I had faith that God would show me.

I had the pen and paper, and God would have to guide and help me with the content. I literally sat down and started writing. God led me to the Bible references in a concordance, and as I dwelt on Him, He prompted me with the themes to use and enabled me to write the words and phrases as they flowed into my brain.

I had a real rekindled yearning to tell others about Jesus and about what God had laid on my heart. God was saying, "Write it down so that others can read it."

It is truly humbling – everything pales into insignificance – when we are able to really understand and dwell on God, Jesus and the Holy Spirit. All three are real persons, living now, loving us and caring for us, supplying our needs. When such love as this is poured over us, how can we not become worshipful and thankful and just awestruck by who God is and what He is doing for each one of us on a daily basis?

Entering into a real relationship with God, through His Holy Spirit, Christians are complete, just as God intended. We need to know all three elements of the Trinity, not choose to leave one out because we can't grasp His purpose!

I have a deep sense of the presence of God; He is so close to me that I just revel in His outstretched arms. The peace of God is real and it surrounds me. There is a complete release of my own human problems, and God's Spirit flows in and through to cleanse and fill me completely.

All Christians receive the Holy Spirit when they accept Jesus into their lives, but it seems that for many the Spirit is not understood and therefore there is a lacking of awareness and spirituality within them. This was certainly the case for me, for I can look back and see the difference over the years since that day.

I knew my human will was going to be a difficult one to be handed over completely to God. It was this element that is the most demanding part of the Christian life. We have to let God deal with it and we need to persevere each day with it.

God is truly marvellous and is continually becoming more and more real to me. It is in fact difficult to describe, even in words, what the indwelling presence of God is like; suffice to say that I am a re-charged and relit Christian.

When we grasp the reality of God and remember His promise that He will be with us in everything, always, then to live our lives for Him and with Him takes us to a closer relationship with Him. Every day, in all we do, God is there with us – at home in the lounge or kitchen, in the office, on the building site, next to the cement mixer or in the car.

For example, something happened regarding God's nearness and protection in an incident in my life in 1996. I travel quite a lot in my work as an Insurance Broker, and it was on one such occasion that I was travelling north to Scotland on the A1. I had made good progress on a beautiful, dry, sunny morning in April. I was considering when to stop for lunch and had decided that the next services would be best so that I could have a good break from driving before continuing on to my first appointment, near Newcastle.

The road was quite clear with only a few slow patches. I was approaching a group of slower vehicles including a very large bulk tanker which was ahead of a line of cars in the inside lane of the dual carriageway. I pulled out to overtake the four cars and the tanker. Having gone past the cars I started to pull alongside the tanker when suddenly, when I was level with the rear of the cab, its right indicator came on!

Imagine my sheer panic! My brain went into overdrive – what on earth should I do now? I was travelling at 70 mph, the tanker probably 50 mph, and there was nowhere for me to turn to avoid the tanker – a crash barrier on my right and the tanker on my left, which by now had crossed the white lane line and was closing in on my space! I sounded my horn but still it kept coming over my way.

My instinct was to accelerate hard and drive half on the grass central reservation and half on the road; it might just give me the seconds I needed to clear the cab. If I had hit the brakes I would have certainly gone under the tanker. So I put my foot hard down on the accelerator and steered onto the grass. For a moment I thought that the plan had worked but then came a huge *bang* and jolt as the tanker collided with the nearside wing mirror and door pillar, destroying the mirror, breaking the windscreen and disfiguring the passenger door.

It was from that moment on that I cannot remember exactly what happened except that the steering wheel seemingly moved by itself! I sensed, more than saw, the next minutes; everything was in slow motion and I am certain, having gone over and over those events, that God's protective hand was there with me in the car.

The first impact had made the car spin around in front of the tanker, which by now was trying to avoid me by returning to the nearside lane again but in doing so hit the car again fully in the rear, demolishing the rear and twisting the hatchback on its pillars. The car was thrown forward and came to rest fifty feet up the road, positioned across both carriageways, and sideways on to the tanker which had still not stopped!

I was conscious although it felt unreal, as though I was somehow merely a passenger in my own car. I was doing nothing, just sitting there; there was no adrenalin flow, no fast heartbeat and no urgency to get out of there. There was complete peace in that mayhem, and I was not at all panicking; I was being cared for. My eyes were not looking out; it was as though I was not being allowed to see what was happening. There was a split second of quietness and stillness, then another almighty, thundering blow to the side of the car, this time at an angle into the rear offside door, breaking the glass and nearly cutting the door in half; it also made my head and neck wrench from side to side and my head slammed into the window of the driver's door.

This third impact of the tanker forced the car backwards at speed, and I can remember being brought back into reality. Realising that the car was going backwards, instinctively I turned around to see where I was going, thinking, "I wonder what it is like to be cut in half," for I knew that traffic was coming up the inside lane! There was, I thought, no other possible end to this incident but to be killed or seriously injured. Then the car crossed the hard shoulder and for a moment I felt nothing, before the car tilted down with the front up in the air.

I was going backwards down a tree-laden grass embankment, at a steep angle! I sat back in my seat, still at peace despite what was happening. Instinctively I put my foot on the brake pedal to stop the car which, after a while, came to rest under some branches and hard against a tree trunk.

There is no doubt that God was with me in that car; there can be no other explanation as to how I survived the crash with only a minor side whiplash injury, no cuts, no bruises and no adrenaline rush or increased heartbeat.

I opened the door and got out, just as though I had parked in a car park, albeit a strange, uphill, grass-and-tree-filled, steep slope! The police and witness both said many times that I was extremely lucky to be alive. In fact the policeman said, "You should not have got out of that; someone must have been looking after you!" How right he was. The car, as you will probably have guessed, was a write-off.

Later in the week, when I was at home, I found out that at the exact time of the accident my parents-in-law were attending a prayer meeting in which people were asked for prayer topics. They asked for a prayer of protection for me on my journey north that day! God answers prayer in ways which we would not imagine, but they are answered in His perfect timing and in His way.

From the moment that I seemed to shut down to the time when my head hit the window, there was someone else controlling that car. I have been asked questions for which I have no physical or human answers. Who steered through the spin? Who took the car out of fifth gear to neutral? How did the tanker damage every panel, including the roof, yet leave no scratch or dent on the driver's door? How was I able to phone the police and my wife from my car phone, when the aerial had been ripped off the body? How was I able to get out of the car and walk up the embankment to the road as though I had just parked and was going for a stroll? Why did I have no adrenalin rush and was not in any kind of state?

The answer must and can only be that my Lord and Saviour, who promises that He will never leave us, is true to His word and had surrounded me with His protective arms.

Having finished the formalities with the police I was able to hire a car and carry on my journey only two hours later, and was able to conduct my business meeting without a problem. I believe I was in a miracle that day and that I witnessed first-hand the amazing power of God.

I now consider myself to be on borrowed time from the Lord and am eager and excited to see what His purpose is for me in His great plan. Don't let anyone tell you that there is no God!

I trust that you will find inspiration from the teaching that unfolds through the chapters of this book and that you will be enabled to come closer to God in your walk with Him, becoming more aware of the amazing, transforming power of God that can be released in your life. I pray that you will experience a real fullness of

God's anointing Spirit, as I have done, as you grow in your personal relationship with Him.

**Peter Bell**
May 2013

# INTRODUCTION

# Don't Keep God in a Box

The Christian life can be described as a journey with God.

At times things don't go so well. We feel down and insecure, but God is there with us, holding our hand even if we cannot feel Him. He is experiencing the emotions with us. There are also times of excitement and joy when we are able to experience the closeness of God and can taste what it is like to be part of God's great adventure as we travel with Him at the centre of our lives, enabling us to be effective for Him.

However, there are many people who have experienced very little of this joy and excitement (or none at all) and are wondering where God is in their lives. They are receiving so much of life's downside and have no real relationship with God; they have really just left Him in the box.

God has a plan for all of us, even when we don't think so. The Apostle Peter said:

> Acts 11:17
> *Who was I to think that I could oppose God?*

He said this when he was explaining to the other disciples what he had felt like after God had told him to go and tell Cornelius about the good news of Jesus. Peter didn't want to go, he didn't think that the Gentiles were to share in the good news of Christ, but despite his own doubts he obeyed God, and through him God not only changed Cornelius' life but also enabled the other disciples to acknowledge that the gospel was not just restricted to the Jews.

We must be careful not to put up man-made barriers to limit God. We must not put God in a box, to be called on only when we need

Him, or make Him fit into our own standard way of worship. God is huge; there is no box large enough to put Him in, but still people try.

We need to listen to God and be obedient to His plans for us and to be guided by Him in all that we do, following his commands and receiving His promises. We are His people, to do His will. If *He* wants to enable us to do His will by empowering us then we should be glad, joyful and praising God, not saying, "This is all too much; God's gone too far this time!"

This book is about living our lives in tune with God and is designed to show that through being closer to God, we will develop practical and spiritually based lives, committed to God and enabling the Spirit of God to be in control of our lives.

I pray that as you read this book, which I believe was God inspired, that He will enable you to look at your journey through life and to have a fresh encounter with Him, as you let Him out of the box and fully into your life, to indwell you and make you on fire for Him.

The down times will still arise, but as you build your relationship with God you will have the strength to endure and realise that He is there with you at all times, no matter what you are doing.

I pray that you will find this book a useful and uplifting experience, that you will discover the real, true, living God as you read these pages, and that you will take Him out of the box and into your heart. Ask Him to guide you as you read.

# Chapter One

# Guidance

## A New Sense of Direction

How many times have you heard about Christian people going their own way, thinking that it is God's way? We are told to trust and obey, but our human wills, our failings and our rational thinking hinder us in this fundamental command of God. It is as though we are saying, "I will do what God says, up to a point, but when it may involve me in something beyond my scope, then someone else can do it."

This attitude will hinder our individual spiritual growth, our relationship with family and friends, our church involvement and most importantly our relationship with God.

> Isaiah 26:4
> *Trust in the Lord forever, for the Lord, the Lord, is the Rock eternal.*

> Proverbs 3:5-6
> *Trust in the Lord with all your heart and lean not on your own understanding; in all your ways acknowledge Him and He will make your paths straight.*

These two verses are really strong in their messages to us. Isaiah emphasises for us to trust in the Lord; he says so three times. It is God in whom we should put our trust, nothing and no one else. If we do this, God is saying that He will make our paths straight. In today's society, many are striving for just this – to have a purpose and a direction for their life.

Guidance is an issue that is not simple; we have to ask God for a discerning heart to hear what He is saying and then to act on it. There are stories of those who have flicked over scripture to find the answer or those who have thought what they were doing was right but hadn't really asked God about it. We all find that 'patiently waiting' becomes frustrating – but God's timing is perfect. If we wait for Him, He will show us the way ahead.

> **Galatians 5:22-23**
> *But the fruit of the Spirit is, joy, peace, patience kindness, goodness, faithfulness, gentleness and self-control. Against such things there is no law.*

Patience is part of the fruit of God's Spirit and is linked to being faithful. We are to have patience and wait on God, having a faithful heart that trusts God.

Guidance is so often a stumbling block, whether we want to change direction in a job or to find new friends or even a spouse! We need to seek the opinion not only of respected Christian friends and our church leaders but above all to seek God's plans by reading the Bible and in prayer.

> **2 Timothy 4:2**
> *Preach the word; be prepared in season and out of season; correct, rebuke and encourage -- with great patience and careful instruction.*

Paul is telling Timothy to have great patience when he is dealing with people. It is the same for us; we want everything done now or tomorrow so that things will happen in our timing, to suit our agenda. This is not the correct way to look at guidance. We need to remember that we are God's servants; we are the instruments through which God does His work on the earth, according to His own timescale.

Sometimes the way that God leads us seems, on human terms, to be wrong because it is not the way that we would have chosen. However, with God we can be sure of His protection and purpose. Many people can testify that when looking back over ten or twenty years they can see how God has led and guided them through their life, which was not so obvious at the time.

**Acts 9:15**

*But the Lord said to Ananias, "Go! This man is my chosen instrument to carry my name before the Gentiles and their kings and before the people of Israel."*

God chose Paul as a significant person to proclaim the good news of Christ to the Gentile world. A most unlikely choice, humanly speaking, but in God's plan just the right person. He was to be an instrument used by God to do His work. We have been saved by God through the death of Jesus and been given eternal life through Jesus' blood. We have no right to put any pressure on God or to put Him into a place which we think is correct for Him in our lives, as another tool to be used when and how we choose.

So what about our human will to do things; can we tame our human desires and will? It is certainly a difficult area to give unconditionally to God. It is probably the most difficult thing at the time of conversion, or soon after, to realise that God wants every part of our lives, every single corner of our being, to be in tune with Him and to be surrendered to do His will.

This is a difficult area to grasp, especially to those seeking Christ. The thought of change, of giving up things that they have been used to doing for a long time, can be a source of worry and doubt. This is where trust and guidance are vitally important.

**Psalm 143:10**

*Teach me to do your will, for you are my God; may your good Spirit lead me on level ground.*

The Psalmist strongly desires to do what is right and acknowledges that it is God who is His only hope.[1] This is a real lesson to us in acknowledging that though we are weak, God is strong, and He will teach and help us. After all, He is our Father. God wants to help us. He wants to be able to fill our lives. He wants to have a relationship that is close and personal.

In the Lord's Prayer we ask God to exert His will on all the earth: "Your kingdom come, your will be done on earth as it is heaven." When we say the Lord's Prayer, do we really mean it? Do we say it out of habit or do we understand the implications of what is being prayed? The Bible is our textbook for Christian life which we need to follow.

---

[1] See Psalm 40:8 for a further example.

One day some Jews came to Jesus to ask Him where His knowledge came from. Jesus said:

> **John 7:17**
> *If anyone chooses to do God's will, he will find out whether my teaching comes from God or whether I speak on my own.*

Jesus said to them that doing God's will is a whole attitude of life. A person who really strives to obey God's commands will welcome the teaching of Jesus and will believe it. Christians should be eager to follow the one person who has done so much for them – not simply with a herd instinct but with a desire to become close friends and to do His will.

When we talk of the will of man we are touching on the very lifestyle and driving force of the individual. Each of us has been made uniquely by God, in His own image.[2] So, as we are made by God, that is even more of a reason why we should bow to His will. Jesus is longing for us to become closer to Him so that we can fully share in all He has to give to us. We are His people and He is our God.

When something is made, whether it is a clay pot or a painting, it has the mark of the maker on it. The style or image of the painting is reflecting the very character of the painter. Artists can say whether a painting is a Picasso or a Renoir – it has their own style. We are made by God in His own image and have the mark of God; we are His. He wants us to do His will. The painter owns the painting and can either keep it, sell it, or destroy it. He has complete control over his work; it is his.

God however is gracious and has given each one of us a free will. We are able to choose, unlike the painting. Although God made us, He has given us the choice of following Him and submitting to His will, or going it alone, disregarding God. This is the fundamental choice facing the person who is seeking to know more about the Christian life. The submission of our selfish lives to God's glorious path of light is one of the most difficult challenges.

From the story of Adam and Eve we can see that man was swayed by the devil to exercise what God had given to man: intellectual choice and rationale. The nature of our being is to please ourselves, but we are called to a higher standard and that is to please God.

---

[2] See Genesis 1:27

**Genesis 2:16,17**
*The Lord God commanded the man, "You are free to eat from any tree in the garden; but you must not eat from the tree of good and evil, for when you eat of it you will surely die."*

God gave Adam a straightforward command and then warned of the consequences of disobedience, but he and Eve chose to listen to the lies of the devil rather than obey.[3] Right at the beginning of the account of man coming into God's world, we read that man was tempted and his will was on test. The choice was there to obey God or eat from the tree of knowledge of good and evil. Man was spoken to by the devil and man understood the logical argument. He considered his choices and decided to do what he thought was a good idea, disobeying God: to eat from the tree.

We can read on in Genesis 3 and see that although God was displeased with Adam and Eve, He didn't destroy them or do anything to harm them. He certainly threw them out of the garden and guarded the tree of life, but in the circumstances God was extremely gracious, despite being obviously grieved in seeing their disobedience. He still loved them, as they were His creation. We can see, not only from the account of Adam and Eve but also from those of Cain and Abel in Genesis 4 and of the Israelites in the wilderness, that man's will had a lot to answer for.

The will of man is strong; it is at the centre of our being. However, that selfish will which has caused countless wrongdoings over the centuries can be tamed and changed.

Although in the Old Testament God was feared by the people, they still disobeyed. In Exodus we read that the people cried out to God when they were in a really bad way, and wanted God to give them food desperately. He did, even though the people grumbled. This demonstrates that God's love for His people is of the deepest kind of love possible – not superficial but a love that is beyond words and is all embracing.

**Exodus 16:12-13**
*I have heard the grumbling of the Israelites. Tell them, "At twilight you will eat meat, and in the morning you will be filled with bread. Then you will know that I am the Lord your God." That evening quail came and covered the camp, and in the morning there was a layer of dew around the camp.*

[3] See Genesis 3:1-7

God had just led the Israelites to safety over the dry sea bed, and now they were grumbling. A God who can push back a sea to let them through would surely not let them die of hunger in the desert, but they may have thought so. What kind of trust had they got? Had their thoughts of God just been superficial? Didn't they have a deeper knowledge of God their creator, who would not let His chosen people perish?

We can learn from numerous accounts in both the Old and New Testaments about the people's insistence on going it alone, deciding that what they were doing was what God wanted them to do or would like them to do.

2 Samuel 11 tells of David's behaviour over Bathsheba and the subsequent murder of Uriah. God was not at all pleased with David.

> **2 Samuel 12:9**
> *Why did you despise the word of the Lord by what is evil in His eyes? You struck down Uriah the Hittite with the sword and took his wife to be your own. You killed him with the sword of the Amorites.*

God doesn't mince His words when He is angry. David should have known much better.

David's son Solomon was a wise man and a great king, but he also did wrong. In 1 Kings 11:1-13 we are told that God had said not to marry the women of the countries around where the Israelites were living because the foreign peoples would turn the Israelites to worship other gods. Solomon, however, loved many other women, which was strongly against God's commands (see verse 6).

God still loved those people and was still able to use them for His work despite their wrongdoing, but He brought them back to Him and made sure that they knew He was displeased. The human will is very strong; it governs the whole being. It is the driving force that spurns us on into whichever way we are heading. If it is not under control, it can ruin us.

How should our will be dealt with and where does God come into the equation? Man's sinful nature sparked by that very first sin in the Garden of Eden has wrought a complete mess to God's creation. We cannot begin to understand or think of His immeasurable sadness when He looks down on His world.

# Chapter Two

# God's Amazing Love

## Breaks Down Barriers

If you make something and someone else smashes it up, a natural outburst would be, "What have you done? That took me hours to make; it was unique!" So what do you think God is saying, right now, about the way in which we are smashing up His unique creation?

Yet despite this God loves us. He made us. He even wants to forgive us! The love of God surpasses our understanding and our knowledge.

> **Ephesians 3:18-20**
> *To grasp how wide and long and high and deep is the love of Christ, and to know this love that surpasses knowledge – that you may be filled to the measure of all fullness of God. Now to Him, who is able to do immeasurably more than all we ask or imagine, according to His power that is at work within us, to Him be glory in the church and in Christ Jesus throughout all generations forever and ever.*

We just can't get our brains around the enormity of God's love for us, which culminated in sending His only son, Jesus, into the world to become a man and to live in a world full of sin. Looking down from heaven day after day, seeing Jesus among sinful man, must have been difficult for Him. God gave us His son to eventually pay the ultimate cost of man's sin, to die in our stead on the cross, to give man a second chance.

God, who had seen the whole of the Old Testament days and who had been let down time and time again by His people, decided in His most loving way to start all over again and allow us to have another go at living the way God intended His unique creation to live.

Look at us now; have we changed? Unfortunately the story repeats itself again. Those same old stumbling blocks, human nature and self will, are still around; they indwell us, they take us over.

When John the Baptist preached about Jesus and told the people that he was coming, he was questioned closely by the Pharisees.[4] John was proclaiming the coming of Jesus and he said he was not worthy to untie His sandals; he recognised the power and the majesty of Jesus. However, many chose to despise Jesus (and John) and from early on plotted to get rid of Him. They decided that Jesus was a troublemaker, interfering with the way they had set to worship God and the way to observe the laws of Moses. They knew how to pray and how to conduct themselves, so why did they need this Jesus telling them to do otherwise? After all, He was gathering unsavoury characters around Him: fisherman, tax collectors and even ordinary people!

Matthew 9:9-13

*As Jesus went out from there, He saw a man named Matthew, sitting at the tax collectors booth. "Follow Me," He told him, and Matthew got up and followed Him. While Jesus was having dinner at Matthew's house, many tax collectors and sinners came and ate with Him and his disciples. "Why does your teacher eat with tax collectors and sinners?" On hearing this Jesus said, "It is not the healthy who need a doctor, but the sick. But go and learn what this means: I desire mercy, not sacrifice, for I have not come to call the righteous, but sinners."*

The Pharisees and the Jewish leaders were trying to distract people from what Jesus was doing and tried to pick holes in His ministry, just because they were jealous of what He was doing and of His following by many people. All the way through the gospels there are numerous times when the Pharisees, Jewish leaders and others questioned what Jesus was doing. Jesus preached many times about Himself and about the importance of doing God's will, so once again the Jews asked a question: "How did this man get such learning without having studied?" Jesus told them plainly why He was saying

---

[4] See John 1:19-27

those things, and the reasons: "My teaching is not my own. It comes from Him who sent me." (John 7:15-16)

Jesus was doing God's will. God sent His son to earth to do His work; therefore Jesus would have been prepared by God, taught by God and enabled by God to do the work. The Jews may have understood the answer but they still chose not to believe what and who was in front of them.

In John 7:25-52 the people talk among themselves about Jesus. But they dismiss Him: "Isn't this the man that they are trying to kill?" (verse 25) "Have the authorities really concluded that He is the Christ?" (verse 26) "But we know where this man is from; when the Christ comes, no one will know where He is from." (verse 27)

If you read the passage you will find that some believed in Jesus and some thought He was a prophet (verse 40). Some were emphatic that "He is the Christ" (verse 41). However there were some who wanted to seize Him there and then. The people were divided and they left Jesus alone.

Even the temple guards realised that there was something special about Jesus, saying, "No one ever spoke the way this man does." (verse 46) The Pharisees were livid that the guards had not brought Jesus back to them. They then demonstrated their worry, their anger and their ignorance:

> **John 7:48**
> *"Have any of the rulers or the Pharisees believed in Him? No, but this mob that knows nothing of the law – there is a curse on them."*

Jesus' teachings were falling on stubborn hearts and the Jewish leaders were getting fed up with Him, but He still loved them. In fact He loved everyone around Him but all they did was to reject Him. They had their own pre-conceived ideas of the type of person that the Messiah would be, what He would be doing and how He would conduct Himself.

Jesus did not fit into their image of the Promised Messiah, so in their eyes He was not the Son of God. How blinkered they were! Even with the evidence staring them in the face and with the physical evidence of His power and miracles, prophecy and healings, they still said no!

It's the same today. The evidence is plain to see both from the Bible and from personal testimonies of Christians, but still people choose not to believe. What is more saddening, people say that they don't need Christianity, that they are living perfectly well as they are, why do they need to have Jesus helping them?

But it is not only non-Christians who are living without the knowledge of the love of God and being assured of eternal life. Many Christians are just going through the motions of a 'Christian lifestyle' without a true and lasting personal relationship with their God. They know it in their heads but not in their hearts, where it will be life-changing.

Every Christian needs to be effective for Christ, playing their part in God's plan to bring this world back from the brink of self-destruction, into the glory of Christ's created world as He had planned it. How does change come about?

> **John 3:31-36**
> *The one who comes from above is above all; the one who is from the earth belongs to the earth, and speaks as one from the earth. The one who comes from heaven is above all. He testifies to what he has seen and heard, but no one accepts his testimony. The man who has accepted it has certified that God is truthful. For the one whom God has sent speaks the words of God, for God gives the Spirit without limit. The Father loves the Son and has placed everything in His hands. Whoever believes in the Son has eternal life, but whoever rejects the Son will not see life, for God's wrath remains on him.*

This is part of John the Baptist's testimony about Jesus. He knew who He was and why He had come to the earth, and he clearly states it.

In the early church, recorded in the Acts, the spread of the good news of Christ was like wildfire. Many people were converted to a true faith in Jesus and the Bible speaks of great numbers committing their lives to Jesus at one time.[5] Those people had put their faith in God; because of what Jesus had done for them, the scales fell from their eyes and the light poured in. Peter and John were going about preaching and healing all over the area. The whole countryside was buzzing with the news of what was happening.

You can imagine what the Jewish leaders and Pharisees thought. They had plotted the death of Jesus and had succeeded in having Him crucified, they had got rid of the one person who was upsetting their settled upright way of life, but all of a sudden it was happening again

---

[5] See Acts 2:41,47

– this time not by one person but by hundreds, no, by *thousands* of people going about telling others what Jesus had done for them as they were encouraged by the Holy Spirit and taught by the disciples.

These leaders of the law just could not contain themselves; it was as though out of the death of one person many more were growing so that there was a steady increase of this gospel message, spreading even further across the country than before. Rather than ending their problems with the death of Jesus, they had multiplied it!

Peter and John were arrested for preaching and were put on trial. However even in the courtroom it was God who was supreme. Acts 4:1-22 tells of the scene but look at verse 13:

> Acts 4:13
> *When they saw the courage of Peter and John and realised that they were unschooled, ordinary men, they were astonished and they took note that these men had been with Jesus.*

What was it that was motivating Peter and John and the other disciples to continue to preach when there was so much pressure – real pressure – to stop? The answer is found in verse 19:

> Acts 4:19
> *Peter and John replied, "Judge for yourselves whether it is right in God's sight to obey you rather than God, for we cannot help speaking about what we have seen and heard!"*

They could have gone back to their quiet, correct beliefs, knowing that Jesus had died and risen for them and that they were assured of eternal life. That would have been a lot easier and safer. There was no need to shout about it, just keep it nice and compact, use the knowledge when they needed and live a decent life with no fuss.

Does that scenario ring true with you? Doesn't this reflect how many Christians are living today? We can be happy to go to church to worship God on Sundays and maybe the mid-week meeting, help with the church fête and attend other functions, but when it comes to volunteering to help with outreach to the community or being involved in the Sunday service or leading a discussion group, we often shy away as we will be out of our comfort zone. When we act like this, we are not realising that once we step up to the mark, Jesus will give us all we need to carry out His work.

We need to wake up and rekindle our Christianity, to become on fire for God. How is your faith? Is your faith motivating you to tell others about what Jesus means to you and has done for you, or do you rely on knowing the facts about Jesus' life on earth, told in the four gospels, and the fact that you can have an assurance of eternal life and that Jesus has come into your heart?

If you do, then look again at those four gospels. What does Jesus say to us all? "Spread the word and tell others!" We can all live Christian lives that are cosy and safe, but what good is that doing for the non-Christians next door, in your community or at work?

We are told to share our faith, not to keep it to ourselves. The good news of Christ is too big to be contained; it needs to take us over and overflow onto those around us. The big question here is, how are we using the knowledge that we have of Jesus?

# CHAPTER THREE

# What is Faith?

Having survived certain death in my car accident[6] made me think of how God is in control of our lives, whether we are aware of it at the time or not. If we have faith in God, what do we really mean by that?

God wants to have full control of our life, but we have to be willing to let Him have every corner of it, no matter how daunting that might feel. God doesn't want ninety per cent or even ninety-nine per cent, He wants one hundred per cent. After all, He has every right to our life; He gave it to us!

This is one of the most difficult areas for Christians. At conversion many know what they should do and hand over their lives one hundred per cent to Christ. However, it is in daily living when it becomes so hard to actually submit everything to God – to get rid of those nasty habits, those secret desires that no one else knows about – but you know that God knows everything about you; nothing can be hidden from Him.

We have all been there. Even, I'm sure, the most devout Christian has at some time had problems in this area. It is, after all, our old friend 'self-will' creeping in. How do we counter this problem; is there an easy answer? There *is* an answer, but it still requires effort on our side.

When we ask God's Spirit to dwell inside and to fill every part of our being we must take the following steps:

- Be truthful with God, owning up to all our secret and maybe not-so-secret things that are not pleasing to Him.

---

[6] See preface

- Ask God to deal with them and put them out of our lives, whatever the consequences.
- Ask God to fill these bad areas with His cleansing love and to blot out any memories of them which could harm our ongoing relationship with Him.
- Pray earnestly that God will help us to endure the consequences and, through being filled with the power of the Spirit, to shine out God's love to others.
- Increase our knowledge and awareness of our faith.

Let's take 'faith' and break it down into manageable sections:

**F** actual
**A** ccessible
**I** ndividual
**T** rustworthy
**H** umbling

## Factual

There are many areas of life where we find factual faith. To sit on a chair requires faith that it will not break and put us on the floor. We know that a chair is made to sit on; therefore our faith in a chair is not usually questioned, unless we can see that the chair is unsafe. Our faith in the chair is a fact, and we sit down. It only takes seconds to see, evaluate and sit.

How does factual faith come into our Christian understanding of faith? We know what Christ has done for us. He died on the cross for us. He rose from the dead victorious. He appeared to His followers after His resurrection. These are all documented, historical facts.

**John 19:17-18**
*Carrying His own cross, he went out to the place of the skull. Here they crucified Him, and with Him two others, one on each side and Jesus in the middle.*

**Matthew 28:5-6**
*The angel said to the women, "Do not be afraid, for I know that you are looking for Jesus who was crucified. He is not here, He is risen, just as He said."*

**John 20:19-20**
*On the evening of that first day of the week, when the disciples were together with the doors locked for fear of the Jews, Jesus*

*came and stood among them and said, "Peace be with you!" After He said this, He showed them his hands and side. The disciples were overjoyed when they saw the Lord.*

We know the facts, and because of these we have knowledge of what happened and we have a faith that Jesus is alive today. If Jesus rose from the dead He is surely the Son of God, as no man could have done what He did. Our rational minds therefore conclude that He is alive today as the Bible does not say that He died again. Christians believe and have faith that He is with us now.

Facts cannot be altered after an event. It was a fact that the tomb was empty, but despite these facts and the ability of the mind to reason out the possibilities of what happened to Jesus and where He is now, still people choose not to believe He rose from the dead and still go their own way. It might be ignorance – they haven't been shown the facts and have not been able to reason for themselves that the only possible answer is a real living Jesus. They have no faith because they have no foundations to base it on. Facts are very important; without them the Christian faith would be on slippery ground.

## Accessibility

Faith is accessible by anyone. There is no need to be super-spiritual, highly intellectual or have a degree in theology. Faith is simple; it is for us to grasp with both hands and to have a sure knowledge that we have access to our maker.

God wants us to access Him continually, and our simple faith makes that possible, for God wants us to be like children, to come to Him as our Father.

**Matthew 19:14**
*Jesus said, "Let the little children come to me, and do not hinder them, for the Kingdom of Heaven belongs to such as these."*

Children, on the whole, are not complicated in the way that they live. They do not ask many questions before doing something that their parents have asked or told them to do. They have faith in their parents, that they would not lead them into danger. If Mum or Dad says, "Sit on the bench, climb those steps, help with the D.I.Y.," they will join in because not only are they responding to parental love but they are trusting in a straightforward way. They have access to their mum's or dad's thoughts, instructions and actions.

Children do not have so many hang-ups or pressures that adults have. A children's world for the under sevens, at least, is a world of 'think and do' – not 'think, evaluate, question and maybe do'.

To have access to something gives us freedom to enjoy what is beyond the access point. If we buy a ticket to gain access to see a beautiful garden, we can fully enjoy that garden which has been lovingly cared for by the owner and which is standing there for us to enjoy, whenever we want to go in. We in the same way have access to God, through Jesus dying on the cross for us. Jesus bore our sins and has given us free access to God whenever we want. We can enjoy His beautiful presence; we have accessibility.

**Romans 5:1-2**
*Therefore, since we have been justified through faith, we have peace with God through our Lord Jesus Christ, through whom we have gained access, by faith into His grace in which we now stand, and we rejoice in the hope of the glory of God.*

**Ephesians 2:17-18**
*He came and preached peace to you who were far away and peace to those who were near. For through Him we both have access to the Father by one Spirit.*

How often do we use the accessibility that we have been given? Is the knowledge that we have it enough for us? Do we fear that going further through the access point may mean that we have to do something as well? We will tackle that question later!

## Individual

Each of us is unique, we are all individual beings, and even twins have certain individuality, although they may look ninety-nine per cent the same on the outside.

Faith is also individual; we all have different degrees of faith. Some have a very strong faith in God and walk closely with Him on a daily basis; others have a weak faith that is easily swayed by worldly things and is difficult to find when pressures start to crowd in.

For many, faith is usually mediocre but sometimes really strong, especially after a church holiday or hearing a dynamic sermon or message. After these events the person's faith is rekindled and strengthened, but after a few days or weeks it may drop back down to 'medium', as the thoughts fade and life gets back to normal.

Humans are very individual, and perhaps it is because we have an instinct to look after number one that we often return to the decision to follow our own self-centred desires – we could call this 'self-will'.

Faith needs to be correctly determined by the individual so that at any one moment our faith in God is not shaken.

> **Luke 17:5-6**
> *The apostles said to the Lord, "Increase our faith." He replied, "If you have faith as small as a mustard seed, you can say to this mulberry tree, 'Be uprooted and planted in the sea,' and it will obey you."*

Jesus has said that it is not the amount of faith that counts; it is whether you have faith itself. An individual's faith can encourage and build up someone else's faith.[7] We can draw strength from each other's faith and the results of that faith in their lives and the lives of those around them. To have faith in God, which in itself is individual, is a building block to enrich and encourage other Christians. God has given us the ability to understand what Jesus has done for us, and that understanding will be different in each person's brain because of their own individuality.

Therefore their own faith, although based on the same firm rock of Jesus, will enable their actions to be different, depending on what God has called them to do for Him.

> **1 Corinthians 12:27-28**
> *Now you are the body of Christ and each one of you is a part of it. In the church God has appointed first of all apostles, second prophets, third teachers, then workers of miracles, also those having gifts of healing, those able to help ,others, those with gifts of administration and those speaking in different kinds of tongues.*

As the body of Christ, Christians are privileged to be given specific jobs to do by God, in order for His word to be spread to others. We are all given individual gifts by God to enable us to use our abilities for God.[8]

We all need to use our gifts and not hide them for fear of embarrassment or of being unable to use them. God gave them to us for His purposes. He will help us to use them for Him. We have to step out in faith. Through having an individual faith we can build

---

[7] See Romans 1:12
[8] See also Romans 12:4-8

each other up and grow ourselves in the work that God wants us to do.

## Trustworthy

Faith and trust go hand in hand; you cannot really have faith in someone or something unless your trust is complete. To put trust in something means that there has to be good judgement and a clear understanding of what you are doing.

If you want to invest some money it would be foolish to go to a complete stranger in the street and say, "Take this money for me and invest it in what you think best, and I will contact you in a few years." The stranger will either think he is dreaming and take the money – it is then a gamble as to whether you will ever see it again – or the stranger will think that you have a somewhat odd grasp of investment and leave you alone.

The investor has to make sure that the place and person to which he entrusts his money is as safe as it can possibly be. That will be determined by personal recommendations, by reading the investment prospectus and by talking to the fund managers.

When the investor is satisfied with his findings, he will make the investment, placing his full trust in that fund and its managers; after all, they have full control of his money. We can find a parallel between what the investor does and what we as Christians should do when we consider our faith and its trustworthiness. When you say that you have faith in God, do you really believe that you are putting one hundred per cent trust in God? What has made you trust Him? It could have been an emotional impulse at a large meeting when you went forward, following a sermon, with a tide of people, not really knowing what you were doing. Everyone else seemed to be happy about it so you decided it was the right thing to do.

Your trust in God at the time of your conversion was a step of faith. It takes a great deal to dump your old life with all those things that you used to do, that you enjoyed doing but that in God's eyes were wrong. You made a decision then to follow Jesus, to say, "Yes I believe in what Jesus did for me on the cross. I want to have my life filled with Jesus, doing what He wants me to do, living a new life for Him."

That statement is one of trust; you are putting your full trust in Jesus. When you said yes to follow Christ, you may well have had the gospel explained to you, either on a one-to-one basis or through a speaker in a large meeting or by your local minister; but however you initially came to Christ, quite soon after you would have been encouraged to read the Bible to see what God was saying to you personally.

You could read the accounts of Jesus' life on earth and of His death and resurrection and be able to base your trust on what you had read and upon the truths stated. After reading there is a process of evaluating and deciding what to do about it for yourself. When you said yes to Jesus, you were certain that it was a good, safe, wise and trustworthy decision. You realised who should be in control of your life and that without Him you would make a complete mess of things, going your own way to eventual destruction. Our faith is therefore full of trust in God our maker. There is no other greater person to put our trust in.

**Psalm 125:1-2**
*Those who trust in the Lord are like Mount Zion, which cannot be shaken but endures forever. As the mountains surround Jerusalem, so the Lord surrounds His people both now and for evermore.*

This is such a strong picture of trust and underlines what happens when we put our trust in God; we cannot be shaken!

**Nahum 1:7**
*The Lord is good, a refuge in times of trouble. He cares for those who trust in Him.*

This is a certain promise from God, and one which we can take as encouragement as we live our lives for God.

Jesus said to His disciples:

**John 14:1**
*Do not let your hearts be troubled. Trust in God; trust also in me.*

He comforted them with these words when He was only days away from His own death! We have such a gracious and caring God that even when at a time of despair and anguish, that must have been felt by Jesus, He still had time to calm His disciples down and to just show them that putting their full trust in God would be an enormous help to them.

## Humbling

People do not like to be humbled, especially if it is in a group of friends or associates. It seems to destroy the person's sense of self-importance, of knowing how they stand and relate to others. We don't like to have our ego undermined. Our human nature is to hold ourself in a certain manner, looking all right outwardly, even if we are not and have inner turmoil which is eating away at us.

Faith is humbling, as we can learn from the life of Moses. Moses was a great man of God, a person whom God used mightily, despite leading the Israelites for many years whilst they grumbled against God. Moses was a leader, a man of God, yet he was the humblest man on earth.[9] He had a massive faith in God, yet God made him humble. He could have had an ego trip, being spoken to by God repeatedly, being enabled to do things such as making water flow out of a rock and drying up the Red Sea. He could have used his position as a leader to demand all kinds of things. Moses knew that nothing that he did was of his own doing. He knew that God was totally in control, and that was why he was humbled.

Moses had faith in the real God who had revealed Himself to him and whose work he had seen closely. He had been in the presence of God on at least two occasions and had had an experience like nothing else on earth.

> **Exodus 3:2**
> *There the angel of the Lord appeared to him in flames of fire from within the bush. Moses saw that though the bush was on fire, it did not burn up.*

> **Exodus 34:5**
> *Then the Lord came down in the cloud and stood there with him and proclaimed His name, the Lord.*

Just like we stand with our friends, the Lord stood with Moses. It must have been overwhelming for him – he had spoken to God, he knew how awesome God is – but look what he said:

> **Exodus 34:6-7b**
> *The Lord, the Lord the compassionate and gracious God, slow to anger abounding in love and faithfulness, maintaining love to thousands, and forgiving wickedness, rebellion and sin.*

---

[9] See Numbers 12:3

Paul, writing to the Ephesians, urges them to be completely humble and gentle.

**Ephesians 4:1-2**
*As a prisoner for the Lord, then, I urge you to live a life worthy of the calling you have received. Be completely humble and gentle; be patient, bearing with one another in love.*

With our faith giving us our knowledge and trust in God, we can learn to be humble and can ask God to help us with it. To be humble is difficult for us; we have so many things going on in our busy lives. It means that we need to rid ourselves of our pre-conceived ideas of what we want from God. We have to put away our shopping lists of what we think we ought to have.

God loves us and will give us more than we can ever imagine, if only we would humble ourselves and come to Him and surrender ourselves totally to Him. God just wants us as we are, His children, to come to Him with an open heart and mind, for Him to speak to us and to give us a new heart.

**Ezekiel 36:26-27**
*I will give you a new heart and put a new spirit in you. I will remove from you your heart of stone and give you a heart of flesh. And I will put my Spirit in you and move you to follow my decrees and be careful to keep my laws.*

To become humbled by our faith is in fact a glorious thing; we just let go of our own built-up ways and thoughts and put every part of our lives into God's hands, letting Him take over, control us and use us. It is so wonderful that it is nearly impossible to describe in writing, except to say that it is 'heaven on earth'.

As you become aware fully of what God has done for you and what He has promised He will do for us, you can appreciate and understand Paul's statement:

**Philippians 1:21-23**
*For me to live is Christ and to die is gain. If I am to go on living in the body, this will mean fruitful labour for me. Yet what shall I choose? I do not know! I am torn between the two: I desire to depart and be with Christ, which is better by far but it is more necessary for you that I remain in the body.*

Jesus was asked in Matthew 18:1, "Who is the greatest in the kingdom of heaven?" In answer, he explained the importance of being childlike in our attitude towards God:

**Matthew 18:4**
*Therefore whoever humbles himself like this child is the greatest in the kingdom of heaven.*

**Matthew 23:12**
*For whoever exalts himself will be humbled, and whoever humbles himself will be exalted.*

This is a lesson for us with our human pride; we need to strive to let God control us, to put God in the driving seat. This will allow things to go much better because we have our instructor and teacher with us all the time. We may have passed the test but we still have the L plates. We are always learning from the instructor.

**James 4:10**
*Humble yourselves before the Lord, and He will lift you up.*

This is a wonderful promise of God,[10] acknowledging our humbleness and lifting us up. Can you imagine how it feels to be lifted up by God, the creator of the world? Through our faith in God we should realise that we need to be humble before Him; He can then work through us in a much more powerful way. We are God's instruments. Let's allow Him to use us fully.

---

[10] See also 1 Peter 5:6

# Chapter Four

# God, Jesus and the Holy Spirit

## How do they fit together?

Faith is multi-faceted but has a strong sense of belonging. We belong to God, we have faith in God. However, if we have faith in God, where do Jesus and the Holy Spirit come into the picture? God the Father, Jesus the Son and the Holy Spirit are all necessary, for they make up the Holy Trinity. They are inseparable but each of them is individual and has a part to play in our Christian life.

God is our creator. He was at the beginning of time for He made everything. Nothing existed before He made it, but God has always been; He has existed forever and will exist forever.

But who is God? This is a big question that we can only begin to answer by looking at what He has revealed to us in His word, the Bible; our human minds are not big enough to comprehend His complexity and hugeness. But let's explore a little of what the Bible tells us about Him. For the rest we will have to wait until we see Him face to face in our eternal home with Him in heaven; then all will be revealed.

In Genesis we encounter God for the first time. He had decided that He would make a beautiful place – the universe with the world in it – in which to put His ultimate creation of man and woman. He accomplished this and He saw that it was good.[11] God was content that He had finished what He had planned and then on the seventh day He rested from all His work. God made all things and loved them

---

[11] See Genesis 1:31

and cared for them, giving man and woman the amazing garden to live in.

However, the beauty was damaged by sin in the form of the devil coming into the garden and tempting the man and woman so that they disobeyed God and ruined His plans. This resulted in God banishing them from the garden because of what they had done – but He still loved them.

This is the start of the story of man's sinfulness and rebellion against God, which hurts God terribly as He made us and still loves us, despite our sinful nature. God is one who promises us so much and will fulfil those promises.

All through the Old Testament we can read of the struggles of the Israelites as they battled with their enemies, but God looked after them and brought them through the trials because He cared for them. They grumbled a lot against God, and it is amazing that He continued to do things for them. God was determined He could once again care for His creation in a beautiful place, but the stumbling block was sin – a huge blot on God's creation. God knows all about us; He could see what was going to happen and therefore could develop His plan to get humans back on track.

God used His prophets to foretell what His plans were going to be. Isaiah foretold the birth of Jesus and that he would be called God and Father as well as Jesus.

> **Isaiah 9:6**
> *For to us a child is born, to us a son is given and the government will on his shoulders and he will be called, Wonderful Counsellor, Mighty God, Everlasting Father, Prince of Peace.*

> **Isaiah 40:28**
> *Do you not know? Have you not heard? The Lord is the everlasting God the Creator of the ends of the earth. He will not grow tired or weary, and his understanding no-one can fathom.*

God's purposes will not be stifled; He will enable His plans to come to fruition, and therefore when we come to the New Testament we read in the gospels about God sending His only son to earth as a baby, which had been foretold by Isaiah. God gave His creation a second chance. Jesus was God's rescue plan for God's world.

Jesus is both fully human and fully divine for He is God, as part of the Holy Trinity. John explains to us, using another name for Jesus: the Word.

**John 1:1,14**
*In the beginning was the Word, and the Word was with God, and the Word was God. He was with God in the beginning ... The Word became flesh and made his dwelling among us. We have seen his glory, the glory of the one and only Son, who came from the Father, full of grace and truth.*

In these verses we can see that Jesus is divine and with God. Jesus existed before everything and was with God. He is a distinct individual sharing His divinity as part of God; the two are one. In the second verse it underlines the fact that Jesus was a human being (as He became flesh) and that He made His dwelling (his home) among us. Our God came from heaven to live on earth, with all its problems and issues, and became a frail human with all the emotions and needs that we have.

There are verses in the Bible that tell us that Jesus displayed human emotions.

### SORROW

**Isaiah 53:3**
*He was despised and rejected by men, a man of sorrows, and familiar with suffering.*

### ANGER

**Matthew 21:12**
*Jesus entered the temple area and drove out all who were buying and selling there. He overturned the tables of the money changers and the benches of those selling doves.*

### LOVE

**John 13:34**
*A new command I give you. Love one another. As I have loved you, so you must love one another.*

### COMPASSION

**Mark 8:2**
*I have compassion for these people; they have already been with me three days and have nothing to eat.*

NEED OF SOLITUDE

**Mark 1:35**
*Very early in the morning, while it was still dark, Jesus got up, left the house and went off to a solitary place, where he prayed.*

SLEEP

**Luke 8:22-23**
*One day Jesus said to his disciples, "Let's go over to the other side of the lake," so they got into a boat and set out. As they sailed, he fell asleep.*

SUFFERING

**Mark 8:31**
*He then began to teach them that the Son of Man must suffer many things and be rejected by the elders, chief priests and teachers of the law, and that he must be killed and after three days rise again.*

Through all these emotions we can recognise the human side of Jesus and therefore have a closer relationship with Him as we also experience those same emotions.

God loves us so much that He sent His only son to die for our sins in our place, on the cross. Jesus was the ultimate sacrifice. When Jesus had finished His time on the earth, had risen from the dead and had appeared again to His disciples, He didn't just say, "Goodbye, you can get on with it now. I showed you how." No, He left someone with them, His Holy Spirit, who is also with us and in us today.

**John 14:15-17**
*If you love me, you will obey what I command, and I will ask the Father, and He will give you another Counsellor to be with you for ever – the Spirit of Truth.*

Jesus was not going to leave His followers in the lurch with no one to help them grow in their Christian lives or to help them build up His Church. It was His Spirit who enabled the disciples to begin their work in spreading the gospel to the known world. These men were fishermen and ordinary people, not teachers or scholars. Without the Spirit helping them they would have got nowhere. The book of Acts chronicles the start of the early church and begins with the apostles being empowered by the Holy Spirit.

In Acts 2, Peter explains that what is happening is all part of God's plan.

Acts 2:14-16
*Then Peter stood up with the Eleven, raised his voice and addressed the crowd: "Fellow Jews and all of you who live in Jerusalem, let me explain this to you; listen carefully to what I say. These people are not drunk, as you suppose. It's only nine in the morning! No, this is what was spoken by the prophet Joel..."*

Peter also underlines the fact that the Holy Spirit comes from the Father.

Acts 2:33
*Exalted to the right hand of God, he has received from the Father the promised Holy Spirit and has poured out what you now see and hear.*

When we became Christians and accepted Christ into our lives, His Holy Spirit came into our hearts to dwell within us. The Spirit of truth enables us to understand more about God. He teaches us the right way to live, how to draw on the power of God in order to enable us to be effective in spreading His word, and how to combat our human nature and desires.

We are told to put off the desires of the sinful nature:

Galatians 5:16-18
*So I say, live by the Spirit and you will not gratify the desires of the sinful nature. For the sinful nature desires what is contrary to the Spirit and the Spirit what is contrary to the sinful nature. They are in conflict with each other, so that you do not do what you want. But if you are led by the Spirit, you are not under the law.*

God loves us so much that He not only sent Jesus to help us but also left His Spirit with us, to counsel us in the ways of God and to comfort us just as Jesus comforted those in need around Him. The Spirit of God is not only found in the New Testament but throughout the Bible.

Genesis 1:2
*Now the earth was formless and empty, darkness was over the surface of the deep, and the Spirit of God was hovering over the waters.*

The Spirit has been present since the beginning of time because He is God's Spirit; He is a part of God, the third part of the Trinity.

**Psalm 139:7-10**
*Where can I go from your Spirit? Where can I flee from your presence? If I go up to the heavens, you are there. If I make my bed in the depths, you are there. If I rise on the wings of the dawn, if I settle on the far side of the sea, even there your hand will guide me; your right hand will hold me fast.*

The Spirit is everywhere. He is all powerful, as God is, and God has given His Spirit to each one of us.

**Isaiah 44:3**
*For I will pour water on the thirsty land, and streams on the dry ground. I will pour out my Spirit on your offspring and my blessing on your descendants.*

God wants us to have His Spirit in abundance, in order to equip us, His people, to do His work on earth. Have we ever considered why God has given us His Spirit personally? We may know full well why He spoke to His disciples and told them He was leaving the Counsellor with them, but do we appreciate the full significance of His words?

**John 14:25-26**
*All this I have spoken while still with you. But the Counsellor, the Holy Spirit, whom the Father will send in my name, will teach you all things and will remind you of everything I have said to you.*

Jesus said that the Spirit would remind them of what He had said. How often in our lives do we have to be reminded about what other people have said? Many times occur when we say, "I'm sorry, I forgot what you said," or, "If I don't write this down, I will never remember it."

We are bombarded with so many words, that to remember them all would be impossible. This is the same with spiritual things; even if we are good at memorising Bible verses, it would be no mean feat to memorise the entire Bible. We have the written word of God, and through reading it God speaks to us, but it is the Spirit within us who prompts us to grasp what is being said and helps us to understand and to recognise what we should do in each situation.

When we are seeking guidance from God on a certain issue, a passage or verse may come into our minds. That is the Spirit reminding us of what Jesus is saying to us. Although we cannot physically see Jesus, we know through our faith that He is always with us, for He said He would be.

> **Matthew 28:20**
> *Surely I am with you always, to the very end of the age.*

The Holy Spirit enables us to sense the very presence of God in our everyday lives. The closer we get to God in our personal relationship with Him, through prayer and Bible reading, the more effective we will become. Enoch was close to God, and one day when walking in God's presence, God took him to be with Him. How marvellous Enoch must have felt to be taken into God's presence, like going into a friend's home!

> **Genesis 5:24**
> *Enoch walked with God. Then he was no more, because God took him away.*

God used the prophet Joel to tell us what He was going to do.

> **Joel 2:28-29**
> *And afterwards, I will pour out my Spirit on all my people. Your sons and daughters will prophesy, your old men will dream dreams, your young men will see visions. Even on both men and women, I will pour out my Spirit in those days.*

> **Joel 2:17-18**
> *Then you will know that I, the Lord your God dwell in Zion, my holy hill. Jerusalem will be holy; never again will foreigners invade her. In that day the mountains will drip new wine and the hills will flow with milk. All the ravines of Judah will run with water. A fountain will flow out of the Lord's house and will water the valley of acacias.*

God's Spirit was being given to men to enable His word to proceed across the earth. His Spirit is being used to refresh His people. The fountain flowing out of the Lord's house is a symbol of a stream of blessing from God which engulfs His people and rekindles the fire within them. When God's Spirit reminds us of what Jesus said and prompts us to understand His word more fully, we can then see that the Holy Spirit is a person living within us who wants us to fully appreciate what God has done for us, and is doing, and will be doing. His Spirit is not to be ignored! He is an integral part of the Trinity and of our Christian lives. The Spirit enables us to live in step with God's will.

Let's recap. God the Father, the creator of the world and our own maker, loved us so much as to send His Son Jesus into the world – to die for us; to take our sins onto Himself; and to give us the opportunity of having eternal life with Him. Jesus conquered death, rose from the dead and ascended into heaven, but He left with us on earth His Holy Spirit to help us and instruct us.

Through Jesus we have access directly to God, and through His Spirit we have a constant source of help and guidance, which enables us to do God's work on earth. Our relationship with God will grow and develop as we grasp the truth that we are part of the intimate relationship of God the Father and Jesus, His son, and are indwelled by his Holy Spirit.

John 14 tells us that when Jesus was explaining to His disciples about the Holy Spirit and the relationship between Jesus, God and the Holy Spirit, some of them did not fully grasp the fact that Jesus was God in visible form; when the Holy Spirit would be sent to be with them, then they would understand what He had been saying.

> **John 14:20**
> *On that day you will realise that I am with my Father and you are in me, and I am in you.*

This tells us that Jesus is in God; they are one. We believe in Jesus, trust Him and are with Him; and Jesus, in the form of the Holy Spirit, is dwelling in us. Surely that is an amazing fact that we need to cherish and understand. The three facets of God, within the Trinity, fit together perfectly and are strong and firm. They are mighty and glorious, each having a divine purpose for us in our lives.

We are a part of that relationship, and we can develop our relationship with God daily as a result of it.

# Chapter Five

# Communication is Vital

With the Holy Spirit dwelling in us, communication to God becomes a natural and exciting prospect to the Christian. Through our prayers and by reading the Bible we will not only be able to speak to God but allow God to speak to us.

Jesus taught us how to pray in Matthew 6:9-13. He talked about praying to His Father many times; He kept a close dialogue with God. This is not surprising as Jesus had been sent to earth by God, to do God's will. It was essential that He kept in touch and, indeed, showed His disciples by example how and when prayer was needed.

If we have been given instructions by our employer or church leader to go to another part of the country to carry out those instructions, it is essential to telephone or email the person who has sent us, to give them a progress report and to ask for any further instructions, or to ask for help on the subject. We would keep in touch because it's our way of being kept informed.

It is the same in our prayer life as Christians. We need to keep in constant touch with God, to thank Him for the answers to prayer and for what He has done for us, to ask for His help for others who may be sick or in need of special care. We are also able to ask for anything that we may need to build us up and to strengthen us to do His work.

> Mark 11:24-25
> *Therefore, I tell you, whatever you ask for in prayer, believe that you have received it, and it will be yours. And when you stand praying, if you hold anything against anyone, forgive them, so that your Father in Heaven may forgive you your sins.*

Prayer is our avenue, our open line, to God; and when we pray Jesus hears us and will be our communicator to Him. Our prayers are always heard. When we speak, God hears, but He may not answer straight away.

We find this to be difficult sometimes, especially if we want to have an answer by return! We are to be patient and to persevere in prayer. God will answer in His own time, when it is right for us. In the meantime we are to pray constantly. In Luke 18, Jesus illustrates this for us with the parable of the widow who begged for justice from a judge; then He explains:

> **Luke 18:7-8**
> *And will not God bring about justice for his chosen ones who cry out to Him day and night? Will He keep putting them off? I tell you, He will see that they get justice, and quickly. However when the Son of Man comes, will He find faith on the earth?*

Prayer is a two-way process. We can know God is right there with us.[12] With that knowledge we can be certain that God is ready and waiting to hear us. We need to come to God in prayer with our hearts open to him having already asked him to forgive those things that we have done wrong and which may cloud our relationship with Him. We need to be in an attitude of humility and expectancy, so that when we pray to Him, He can speak to us.

Be joyful when you come to pray,[13] for you are speaking to your Heavenly Father, your maker. Isn't that concept just overwhelming for our tiny minds to grasp? We may be scared if we have to talk to our boss or to the local mayor, or completely overcome with nerves if we are ever in the presence of the Queen, but we have access through Jesus to come to God in prayer knowing that we are speaking to the King of Kings. He is over all nations and all kings and queens; they all bow down to Him.

We are able to call Him our Father. We need not be nervous, frightened or scared. We are His children; He loves us and wants to talk to us. Just as a parent loves their children and adores talking and being with them, so too is God waiting and wanting to talk to us and listen to our prayers. We are to treat prayer as conversation, not set pieces or lists of things that we think we ought to pray about or that everyone prays about. It is essential, of course, to remember other people's needs and areas of the world that do need our prayers for peace, but we must not neglect just to talk about how wonderful the

---

[12] See Deuteronomy 4:7
[13] See 1 Thessalonians 5:16-18

day is or the flowers look, or to thank God for rain or the brightness of the moon.

Thanking and praising form a good deal of prayer time. We need to praise God because without Him there would be nothing.[14]

> **Psalm 33:1-5**
> *Sing joyfully to the Lord, you righteous, it is fitting for the upright to praise Him. Praise the Lord with the harp, make music to Him on the ten stringed lyre. Sing to Him a new song, play skilfully, and shout for joy. For the word of the Lord is right and true, He is faithful in all He does. The Lord loves righteousness and justice, the earth is full of His unfailing love.*

The Psalms are a source of an immeasurable wealth of praises to God. In the above verses, the Psalmist just bubbles over with His gratitude to God for helping Him in many situations. It is good to use the Psalms when praising God ourselves.

Everyone likes to be thanked when they have done something for others, although we need to control any feelings of pride that result from the thanks. If we were being asked continually to do things either in church or away from church, and we willingly did them but received absolutely no thanks, we would become sad and maybe depressed and would probably end up saying no to everything that we were then asked to do. Our God is not like that. Although He might not receive the amount of praise due to Him and may well be sad at our apparent disregard for Him, He still answers our prayers, supplies our needs and guides us through life.

> **James 5:13-16**
> *Is anyone of you in trouble? He should pray. Is anyone happy? Let him sing songs of praise. Is anyone of you sick? He should call the elders of the church to pray over him and anoint him with oil in the name of the Lord. And the prayer offered in faith will make the sick person well. The Lord will raise him up. If he has sinned, he will be forgiven. Therefore confess your sins to each other and pray for each other so that you may be healed. The prayer of a righteous man is powerful and effective.*

God commanded us to love one another.[15] This is essential in both the church family and the world at large. If we love, we care. If we care, we all share in each other's problems and joys, and as a result

---

[14] See 1 Chronicles 16:23-25
[15] See John 13:34-35

the body of the Church becomes much more meaningful and in tune with each other, ready to do God's work. We therefore need to pray for one another as an essential part of our prayer life. We are also told to love our neighbours.[16]

With these commands we have plenty to pray for and to praise God for. Friends are very precious. A person with no friends is very lonely, becomes easily depressed and has a feeling of not being wanted. Christians not only have the body of Christ, His Church, and fellow believers as friends but also have the greatest friend of all time – Jesus – close beside them.

Through prayer we have an avenue to God along which we can walk all the time. To have a regular prayer time is one of the most useful things that we can have in the growth of our Christian life.

> **Colossians 4:2**
> *Devote yourselves to prayer, being watchful and thankful.*

If this was good for the church in Colossae then it holds true for us today as well. How much do we really devote ourselves to prayer? If we want to find out what God has for us then we have to come to Him and listen and be shown by Him. This may be from a Bible verse or passage being enlightened by God speaking clearly to us, or it may be God's Spirit guiding us to do something or to go somewhere where we will be in a position to hear God's word through someone else.

Faith and prayer go together.

> **Mark 11:20-25**
> *In the morning, as the disciples and Jesus went along, they saw a fig tree withered from the roots, "Rabbi, look! The fig tree that you cursed has withered!" "Have faith in God," Jesus answered. "I tell you the truth, if anyone says to this mountain, 'Go throw yourself into the sea,' and does not doubt in his heart but believes that what he says will happen, it will be done for him. Therefore I tell you, whatever you ask for in prayer, believe that you have received it, and it will be yours. And when you stand praying, if you hold anything against anyone, forgive him, so that your Father in heaven may forgive you your sins."*

If we really believe in the power of prayer and believe that God will answer our prayers, He will. God's promises are not empty. What God says, happens. We may ask if God really does answer our prayers. What proof do we have? We have our own experiences of

---

[16] See Mark 12:29-31

answered prayers but also the evidence of scripture, e.g. 1 Chronicles 5:20.

I remember the first time I realised that Jesus had answered one of my prayers. It was some time ago whilst at school. I had been watching a game of tennis being played by four of the school prefects on the headmaster's tennis court. The court was bounded on one side by a tall, thick, prickly hedge which was so dense that there was little daylight being let through. Having watched for about ten minutes, I realised that I should be on my way to my next class. I got up and started to walk away, when one of the prefects shouted over to me, "We lost a ball earlier in the hedge. Find it for us!"

I was caught between being late for my class or suffering from a prefect's forfeit for ignoring their request. What was I to do? I sent an 'arrow prayer' and asked God to help me find the ball and still be in time for my class. I stood in front of the hedge, plunged both hands into it and pulled the branches apart. Nothing! Where I had made a kind of hole, the light was shining through it and on looking up into the lit area I saw not one but two balls!

I picked them out and for a moment held them, saying a big 'thank you' to Jesus for answering my prayer. I came around to the front of the court and yelled out to the prefects, "I found your ball and another one as well!" and threw them into the court. Their faces were a picture not to be forgotten.

Not only had I found the lost ball but I also arrived at my class just in time. God is true to His promises, and although my example is somewhat mundane, it has served as an important lesson to me and one on which I have been able to lean and remember many times when I have prayed for specific things. That story has also been used to illustrate God's answers to prayer on many occasions when teaching young people about prayer and the way in which God does answer them.

It is important to remember that when God answers our prayers, we should thank Him, for it is very easy to forget to do so, especially when we are caught up in the rush of the day. Without God's help we won't get far so we need to recognise what He is doing for us all the time and give Him our grateful thanks

**Philippians 4:4-7**
*Rejoice in the Lord always. I will say it again, rejoice! Let your gentleness be evident to all. The Lord is near. Do not be anxious about anything, but in everything, by prayer and petition, with*

*thanksgiving, present your requests to God. And the peace of God, which transcends all understanding, will guard your hearts and your minds in Christ Jesus.*

God gives us a peaceful heart when we lay our burdens and fears before Him in prayer. If we are willing to come to Him and confess that we cannot do things ourselves, He will help us. We just need to recognise prayer as a conversation between us and God. We don't have to use fancy language or a special tone of voice. When speaking to God, just be yourself and be natural; it's far simpler![17]

Pray earnestly; have courage to tell God what is on your heart concerning others, and matters which you have kept bottled up. If you have problems, let God know them too and He will help you with them. Praying gives us spiritual power; we are able to harness the power of God through His Spirit.[18]

Prayer is powerful, and to pray is an element of our Christian lives not to be taken lightly. We must be constructive in our prayers and learn from what we hear from God.

**James 5:16**
*Therefore confess your sins to each other and pray for each other so that you may be healed. The prayer of a righteous man is powerful and effective.*

**2 Peter 1:3-4**
*His divine power has given us everything we need for life and godliness through our knowledge of Him who called us by His own glory and goodness. Through these He has given us His very great and precious promises, so that through them you may participate in the divine nature and escape the corruption in the world caused by evil desires.*

We need to exercise discernment in how we pray. To work out a regular structure for prayer and Bible reading is essential. This can of course be augmented by prayer and Bible reading at other times, but to have a daily slot, when you can sit down and study the Bible and pray, is very important if we are to live our lives in tune with God.

Some find time at night, others in the morning or during the day. It is up to you to decide when and where is best. Personally I prefer early morning after breakfast, before I go to work. It is the quietest

[17] See Matthew 6:5-8
[18] See Acts 1:8

time, and I can concentrate on God's word and take time to listen to Him without disturbance from telephones, television, cats or my wife!

To have a pattern of reading the Bible is a good idea, so that a manageable-sized passage can be read and absorbed. There are many good Bible reading notes and books available which have set passages following a theme or topic and include helpful comments. To read the Bible at random is not the best way of approaching God's word, but some people do this and find it useful.

The Bible is our instruction manual on Christian living. It tells us the history of the creation of the earth, God's dealings with His chosen people and the way in which He used men and women in His plan. Since the fall of man in the Garden of Eden, when sin entered God's glorious creation through the failing of Adam and Eve, God set up a rescue plan which can be traced right through the Old Testament.

The Israelites eventually settled in the Promised Land of Canaan, and this was the culmination of many years of ups and downs. God's people were now in God's place, under God's plan and under God's rule. The stage was set for the second phase of God's plan: to bring from the family of King David (who had been a prominent figure in the Israelites' history) a once-and-for-all, supreme sacrifice to complete God's rescue. This was in the shape of Jesus being born in Bethlehem, David's town.

Jesus was to teach men and women of God's ways and was to die on the cross for us, rescuing us from the sin that was inherited by man's failings. God turned sin on its head and gave His son for us. The Bible continues after the four gospels with the letters of Paul and the Acts of the Apostles, showing us aspects of Christian living and other essential truths and insights into how we should be living out our Christian lives. The Book of Revelation, at the end of the Bible, shows us a little of what heaven may be like and looks forward to the second coming of Jesus.

The Bible is a storehouse of information which needs to be used over and over again. We should let God speak to us from His word. After all, it is pointless having an instruction manual and leaving it on the shelf! If we buy a washing machine, do we guess how to use it? No! We read the manual and then use our knowledge to operate the machine effectively.

The same is true of the Bible. We are to study it regularly to learn how we should be living as Christians, pray over what we have read and listen to God's word speaking to us. To use the Bible and prayer effectively will equip the Christian to cope with life's rich tapestry and will build up our faith and personal relationship with God.

# CHAPTER SIX

# Practical and Effective Christian Living

We have gone through some topics relating to our Christian beliefs which are fundamental to our spiritual wellbeing. Perhaps they are very familiar to you; you recognise that you do know these concepts and believe that you are therefore living your Christian life to the full and there is no more for you to do. Others may not be at that point and have been triggered to reassess their lifestyle and understanding of God. Whichever category you are in there is still another vital part of the Christian life that Christians need to face up to and to exercise earnestly: practical Christian living.

It is fine to know, in your mind, what God has done for you, that He works through Jesus and enables your faith and trust, but what are you doing with that knowledge?

We have talked about our own human wills versus God's will and about the amazing love of God and of faith and its various parts. We have outlined the issues concerning God, Jesus and the Holy Spirit and have explored prayer and Bible reading.

However, what do you actually feel now after contemplating the overwhelming and amazing concept of God, in all His glorious majesty? Do you want to know more or are you content to continue as you are, happy with your life and acknowledging in your head these things concerning God?

Are you going to keep God in a box forever? The choice is yours. It is between you and God. I would urge you now to pray to God, your maker, and to ask Him what He wants of you. Surrender your human will one hundred per cent to God, listen to what He says to you, and then act on it.

**Matthew 7:7**
*Ask and it will be given to you; seek and you will find; knock and the door will be opened to you.*

Are you going to just look through the open door that God has opened to you? Or are you going to go through that open door to experience a fresh, new outlook on the Christian life, not just knowing that God is with you but feeling and touching His presence as you walk together?

I came to this point during September 1994. I knew in my mind what God had done and does do for me; but was I really living my life as God wanted? Was I doing everything that God wanted me to do? What else could God do with me if I only let Him?

When you realise that there is so much more that God can do with our lives, this is the time that you become really aware of the might and majesty of God. This realisation should spur us on to want to do as much as we can for God. When I really became aware, and had a refreshed sense, of what and who God is, I was so fired up, wanting to see what God was going to do with me. It was as though I had wasted years of my life, not really knowing what a Christian is to do, not really understanding the true love of God. The penny had suddenly dropped and – wow – I wanted to go for it!

If we take time to read God's word and to dwell in His glory, we become more and more eager to be a real part of His purpose for us. The stumbling block for so many Christians is the transition from a cerebral Christian (knowing all about it and going through the motions of Christian existence) to becoming a dynamic 'doing' Christian (full of love for God and letting Him take full control of their lives).

One of the longest journeys for a Christian is the one from the brain to the heart, from knowledge of God to actual living with God. The lukewarm frame of mind states, "As long as I do what is right, live as I should and how I have been taught, then God will see that I have not done too badly and will be satisfied with my Christian life." God does not reprimand people for existing like that but He just longs for us to be effective and to spread His good news to others. If we keep God in a watertight compartment to be used when we want, it is rather like saying, "Break glass in an emergency." God is Lord of all, King of Kings; we cannot restrain Him, so why do we try?

God is everywhere, knowing all about us. One of the hardest decisions for our human nature is letting go of things, of possessions, memories or our habits, which have been built up for years. Many people keep in their minds opinions which are not at all useful or good to hold on to. It is these areas, along with unhelpful desires for possessions, money, position in society and so on, which crowd out God and what He wants to do for us – which will be far better and more meaningful than anything we could imagine.

It is difficult, especially if we have become set in our ways, to re-think, to start afresh and to alter our lifestyle, because we will bring up all the arguments that come to mind, such as "What will our family and friends think?" "What will our work colleagues think?" "What will our church friends and church leaders think?"

However, if we change our lifestyle, step out in real faith and let God have full control of our lives, whatever happens, God will be with us and He won't let us down.

Will you open the box and free God to dwell with you in every millimetre of your being, even those areas which no one else ever knew existed? That does take courage, but why should you be so self-conscious of what others think? Isn't it far more important to turn that argument on its head and say, "If I call myself a Christian, then I should live as a Christian, all the time with all of my being and all of my life, so that I am strong to do what Jesus has commanded me to do."?

> Titus 2:11-14
> *For the grace of God that brings salvation has appeared to all men. It teaches us to say "No" to ungodliness and worldly passions, and to live self-controlled, upright and godly lives in this present age, while we wait for the blessed hope, the glorious appearing of our great God and Saviour, Jesus Christ, who gave Himself for us to redeem us from all wickedness and to purify for Himself a people that are His very own, eager to do what is good.*

We should be considering what God thinks of how we are living our lives, rather than raising arguments to support why we want to continue as we are. Jesus' disciples certainly did not continue to live as they were. After they were called by Jesus and followed Him, and saw and learnt from His ministry, they became aware of who Jesus was and what He had done for them.

After His death and ascension, the disciples where assured that the Holy Spirit would be with them as their counsellor.

**Luke 24:52-53**

*Then they worshipped Him and returned to Jerusalem with great joy. And they stayed continually at the temple, praising God.*

This shows us that the disciples just wanted to worship and praise God for everything that He had done for them. They knew that He had physically gone from them, but they also believed and trusted in His word, that the Holy Spirit was with them.

**Acts 2:1-4**

*When the day of Pentecost came they were all together in one place. Suddenly a sound like the blowing of a violent wind came from heaven and filled the whole house where they were sitting. They saw what seemed to be tongues of fire that separated and came to rest on each of them. All of them were filled with the Holy Spirit and began to speak in other tongues, as the Spirit enabled them.*

This was to impact mightily on the early church. It was like having a rocket put underneath them. God's timing was perfect; to gather all the disciples together would have been straightforward, but why not wait until the day of Pentecost when they would all be together, on the first day of the week (and it was also the beginning of a Feast week)?

The power of the Spirit enabled them to get really moving, to use the knowledge they had received to tell others about Christ under God's direction. They were literally transformed into new people, eagerly wanting to do what God wanted. They had an incredible yearning to spread what they had found to be life-changing. They had found a new boldness.

**Acts 4:29**

*Now, Lord, consider their threats and enable your servants to speak your word with great boldness.*

What do you want to happen in your life? Do you want to have all that God wants to give you, or are you content just to sit back and continue living in the routine that you have at present?

**Titus 3:14**

*Our people must learn to devote themselves to doing what is good, in order that they may provide for daily necessities and not live unproductive lives.*

Let's not be complacent; we are seeing the growth of other religions, both around the world and in our own country. There has been discussion about the UK church being in decline, about empty churches – and the media has highlighted some unfortunate happenings within the church.

Are we going to sit back and let the church continue to fall into a state of decay, until it lacks authority to speak to the nation and draw people to Jesus? Surely we should stand up for Jesus and turn the church's image around; focus on His cross and what He has done; go out and announce the good news, wholeheartedly seeking God's plan for each of us and each of our church groups.

Churches should be journeying together in the growth and spread of the good news. Too many churches are doing their own thing, thinking that they are doing things the right way. Surely we should all be asking God to show us what and how He wants the Church to move. If we have a clear purpose, which we have in Christ, we should steer a clear course with boldness and courage.

The Christian life is not all sweetness and light. Jesus never said we would have an easy ride, but He did promise that He would never let us into a situation in which we would have no way out.[19]

Temptations, persecutions and distractions will continue, and these elements will try to crowd into our lives, make us go back into our rut and exist as before: a nice cosy Christian! The devil can't stand a Christian who is actually working or doing the will of God. Satan would much prefer us to just exist and not do anything at all. If we are hard at work, he has got to be as well!

> **John 15:20**
> *Remember the words I spoke to you, "No servant is greater than his master. If they persecuted me, they will persecute you also. If they obeyed my teaching, they will obey yours also."*

Paul was concerned for the Thessalonians when they were going through a sticky patch, so he sent Timothy to strengthen and encourage them, so that they would not be unsettled.

> **1 Thessalonians 3:6-7**
> *But Timothy has just now come to us from you and has brought news about your faith and love. He has told us that you always have pleasant memories of us and that you long to see us, just as we long to see you. Therefore brothers, in all our distress and persecution we were encouraged about you because of your faith.*

---

[19] See 1 Corinthians 10:13

Through persecution, in whatever form, we can come closer to Christ, because He is near to us and we can reach out and hold His hand. He won't let us fall. We can praise Him for His support and love for us. One of my favourite verses says, "I can do everything through Him who gives me strength."[20] Jesus is with us, strengthening us; we will be built up in our faith.

Before you read any further, I invite you to say the following prayer if you really want to change out of the rut, to free God from the box and to give your life, will and human nature totally, one hundred per cent to God, for Him to use as He wants, to let God control your life.

> *Dear God,*
>
> *I want to thank and praise you for doing so much for me, for loving me despite my failings. I recognise that I have not let you have one hundred per cent of my life up to now. I ask that you will forgive me for keeping parts of my life to myself and only living my Christian life on my terms.*
>
> *Lord, fill me now, one hundred per cent, and use my life as you want to. Strengthen my faith and help me to live for you, from now on.*

If we get out of the rut, onto fresh ground, we can travel faster and also discover a whole lot more about God and of what He has in store for us. Let me tell you some areas in which I have found a difference, with a new perspective and outlook on God. To change the way we have done things in the past gives us a new lease of life; this is true in our Christian lives. We should strive to be more effective in the following areas, which will give us a renewed vigour.

## 1. Bible reading

I have always found daily Bible reading notes helpful.[21] However, it can become just a daily habit with nothing really being learnt from the passage; God is not allowed to speak to us. What I have found to be rewarding is to imagine myself actually there in the story being read, actually in the group around Jesus, or in the wilderness, or before the Jewish leaders, or in Egypt with Joseph. If we can take part

---

[20] 1 Philippians 4:13

[21] If you do not currently use Bible reading notes, you might try 'Every day with Jesus' by CWR, or 'Daily notes' by Our Daily Bread

in what we are reading, the passage will come alive and we will really understand why the account is there for us to read, and we will then learn from it. Ask Jesus to help you in this and praise Him for the freshness of the Bible words. We can learn new things every time we read the word of God.

Secondly, dwell in the passage, or come back to it. Note down any verses that strike you as really relevant to an area of your life, or which have come out of the passage at you. It could be that God is saying something to you, and it is best to write it down so that you can pray over it and ask for God's guidance.

As well as regular Bible reading of set passages, meditation on scripture really does help one to learn more about God, especially the Psalms. Meditate, pray and then have a time of waiting for God to speak to you.

The wonders of His word are there for us to enjoy and to learn from. Many times we find that either during church services or meetings (or our own Bible reading times) we will read or hear a passage which is very familiar, be it from one of the parables or the Sermon on the Mount or the Easter/Christmas stories. When we hear the passage, do we turn off because we have heard it all before? Or are we attentive to hear what God wants to tell us through the passage at that moment?

Scripture, when read with God's guidance, can come alive. We will read and understand passages that we have read time and time again and have never really grasped the true meaning of before. This has been true for me. Passages are more meaningful and more significant than ever before. The Bible is a tremendous source of information and divine knowledge.

Some parts of the Bible are more difficult to understand and we may avoid them – some of the prophets, for instance Habakkuk or Haggai, and maybe some of the New Testament letters. However, we need to make time to read these books and letters and ask God to guide us through and to speak to us from them. Titus, I have found, is a storehouse, full of how to live the Christian life. God inspired all scripture; it is 'God breathed'.[22] Therefore He wants us to read all of it in its entirety, not just parts, and to learn from it.

You might consider using Bible study guides. These resources can take you through scripture in manageable chunks, providing

[22] See 2 Timothy 3:16-17

additional background, discussion and questions, helping you to understand and apply what you are reading.

The Bible is an essential part of the armour of God.[23] No one would go into battle without a weapon, and it is the same for us; without the Bible and its knowledge we cannot fight the spiritual battle which God has called us to fight. A Bible is useless if it is left on a shelf, unopened. It might as well have blank pages!

**Colossians 3:16-17**
*Let the word of Christ dwell in you richly as you teach and admonish one another with all wisdom, and as you sing Psalms, hymns and spiritual songs with gratitude in your hearts to God. And whatever you do, whether in word or deed, do it all in the name of the Lord Jesus giving thanks to God the Father through Him.*

Paul is clear in his teaching that without the reading of the Bible we will not be able to have the word of God dwelling in us. It is so important that we learn and teach what God is saying to us. When we took examinations we needed to immerse ourselves in the subject, by reading and re-reading the text books as well as attending lectures. God's word is far more important than any academic achievement, yet it would seem that many Christians do not regard the Bible in the same way. It is, however, our textbook from God to teach us how He wants us to live. Should we not immerse ourselves in the word of God?

**Hebrews 4:12**
*For the word of God is living and active. Sharper than any two-edged sword, it penetrates even to dividing soul and spirit, joints and marrow. It judges the thoughts and attitudes of the heart.*

**James 1:22-25**
*Do not merely listen to the Word and so deceive you. Do what it says. Anyone who listens to the word but does not do what it says is like a man, who looks at his face in a mirror and, after looking at himself, goes away and immediately forgets what he looks like. But the man who looks intently into the perfect law that gives freedom, and continues to do this, not forgetting what he has heard, but doing it, he will be blessed in what he does.*

Therefore do not neglect the word of God, through which He wants to speak to you. When a verse or passage speaks to you, make

---

[23] See Ephesians 6:17

a note of it or try to memorise it. We can use scripture in our prayers to praise God as well as calling upon our renewed knowledge of the word in times when we need encouragement or reassurance. God has given us a vital resource; we need to get to grips with it. If we strive to know God's word more and more we will become more effective as Christians and be able to talk to others with that knowledge within us.

## 2. Prayer

We have already seen why prayer is so vitally important to the Christian, but *how* should we pray? Are there any special ways which are better than others? Jesus told us how to pray when he taught His disciples the Lord's Prayer:

> **Matthew 6:9-13**
> *This, then is how you should pray: Our Father in heaven, hallowed be your name, your kingdom come, your will be done, on earth as it is in heaven. Give us today our daily bread. Forgive us our debts, as we also have forgiven our debtors. And lead us not into temptation, but deliver us from the evil one.*

This pattern was useful for the disciples to have because most of them would not have prayed before and therefore did not know how to pray.

You may find it useful to split prayers into areas which can be used for effective prayer time and can pinpoint certain things, more than just generalising.

- **P** raising
- **R** epentant
- **A** sking
- **Y** ourself
- **E** vents
- **R** esting

PRAISING

It's good to praise God for what He has done for us and others, and it's great to start your prayer time just praising and thanking God. This really puts us into a frame of mind in which we are aware of being in His presence and know that we are talking to God. To praise God following reading the Bible can lead to thanking Him for His word and what we have received from it.

### Repentant

It is important that we ask God to forgive us for anything that we have done wrong. God has said that He will forgive us our wrongdoings and will forget those things forever, but if we don't bring them to Him, we cannot come to be in a right frame of mind to continue our prayers.

> **Jeremiah 15:19**
> *Therefore, this is what the Lord says, "If you repent, I will restore you that you may serve me; if you utter worthy, not worthless words, you will be my spokesman."*

If we are still hanging on to a thought of injustice and are holding it against someone, God does not like it. Thoughts can become deeds, and if we have wrong thoughts we can lead ourselves into trouble. Tell God about them; unload your worries and troubles to Him for He will deal with them.

### Asking

We may find that we use this type of prayer more often than any others. This is common as it's very easy to store up loads of things to put on our spiritual shopping list. God does not say we shouldn't have a long list, but the Bible does say that we need to ask in accordance with God's will.

> **1 John 5:14-15**
> *This is the confidence we have in approaching God: that if we ask anything according to His will, He hears us. And if we know that He hears us, whatever we ask, we know that we have what we asked of Him.*

> **1 John 3:21-22**
> *Dear friends, if our hearts do not condemn us, we have confidence before God, and receive from Him anything we ask, because we obey His commands and do what pleases Him.*

Asking for anything in life may seem easy – but do we mean what we say? If someone says, "What do you want for Christmas?" we may have a genuine item which we have longed for but which is outside of our financial grasp (and may well be outside of the giver's grasp as well!) So we think of a lesser item which is equally something that we would like but not something we would have normally bought for ourselves; that is what we ask for.

How many times have you been faced with this problem when someone has asked you about a Christmas present? The luxury item has gone so we have to scratch around for something that we are not desperate for but if we were to be given it, it would save us buying it and we may use it.

Now let us address the next person who asks us that same question. We have run out of ideas, so our answer is, "Anything really. I am not too sure. I will leave it up to you." The person who wants to know what to give us is no better off, and we will have to rely on their judgement – possibly socks again!

When we come to God asking Him for things, we need to have an ordered list of items which may include such things as asking for help for people's problems, healing for others, peace in the world and for the spreading of the gospel. All these things are genuine but to be even more effective it would be good to be more specific. God knows what we want because He knows us, but so that you can pray earnestly, find out a little more about the problems around the world, about missionaries that your church support. Ask how the health of the elderly members of your church is and any particular problems that may be involved.

Prepare for prayer; be informed about the needs of those you know, world situations, items for praise. Specifics are so much better, especially if you are praying in a group, because you can pray more effectively when you can talk to God about the subject. It is the same as when you are talking to your friends about the needs of others – they can understand and discuss the issue.

### YOURSELF

It is important that we put God and others before ourselves as it allows us to be humble before God, putting our needs after those of others. Jesus was a living example of caring for others.

Consider, for example, the feeding of the five thousand (Luke 9:12-17). This was an amazing demonstration of God's power to answer Jesus' prayer and to enable a very practical, caring, loving thing to happen: the provision of a simple, satisfying meal. When we come to prayers for ourselves, these are to be for help in certain areas, for strength to be effective for Christ and simply an opportunity to talk to God about how we are feeling.

Jesus is interested in us and wants to see how we are doing. Just talk to Him and you will be surprised about the things that will pop into your head to say to Him. Our quiet prayers with God can really charge us up. Jesus often told His disciples of things to pray for themselves.[24]

If you have a concordance, turn to the word 'pray' and go through some of the examples. These will help you in your own prayer time.

## Events

There are many Christian events in the United Kingdom each year and there are also events on a smaller scale in our own localities or at our churches. In addition, there are worldwide Christian events which need vital prayer support. If you are able to obtain information on any of these, it will help you as you pray in a general way for the events, that through them God will touch many hearts.

There are many practical needs such as venues, stewards, weather, individual needs, the health of the speaker, the choir, musicians and so on. There are of course spiritual needs concerning the ministry of God's word, the impact on the congregation, the counselling programme and the follow up.

Prayer power behind these events really does matter. The more people who can pray for an event, the more the impact will be on those who have come to listen.

## Resting

Very often there is a tendency to pray and go. We don't give God any time to speak to us or on our behalf. We are not allowing ourselves time to contemplate any of the issues that we have prayed about. So have a time at the end of your prayers to just sit or kneel and wait in the presence of God, resting in His Spirit. I have found this is really uplifting and glorious. During these times I have found that the peace of God flows over me. It is a feeling of sheer glory; it is so difficult to describe.

> **Philippians 4:7**
> *And the peace of God, which transcends all understanding, will guard your hearts and your minds in Christ Jesus.*

---

[24] See Luke 22:40

God wants to speak to us, so why not give Him time to speak directly? A real sense of being in His presence is there, and you will know that you have been praying to a real God and not just to the ceiling of your room!

It may be useful to have a prayer diary, which can be made from a notebook divided into thirty one pages – one page for each day of the month. Divide each page into sections that we have covered, or add more if you wish. Insert topics under each heading which you want to pray about regularly and leave enough room for any special items which may occur that you want to pray about once or twice.

Prayer is a personal thing, but it can help you during your prayer time to help focus on particular areas. The actual amount of time spent in prayer is up to you, but if you are able to put aside space at the same time each day, you will be able to slowly build up a useful period where you are talking to God and also meditating on His word. You may find that ten minutes suits you, but as you get used to spending more time with God you will want to spend longer and longer!

I find that first thing in the morning is best, when it is quiet and the rushing of the day has not started. To be able to spend more time with God allows God to be able to open up His word and to teach and uplift me from it.

Time spent in prayer also enables us to hold others in prayer, and through this I have seen answers to prayer. I have found that since I have become more involved in prayer, God has both rejuvenated my personal prayer life and has been answering my prayers at a rapid pace.

Each person will find the best time in the day and the best place in the house for them to be able to be quiet and talk to God. It will depend on your lifestyle and routine, but I urge you to make time for prayer, even if you are a busy person. Prayer is our lifeline to God. It is an essential part of our Christian life.

Ask God to help you and show you the best place and time. If you get up an hour earlier each day to pray before you go to work, God will give you that extra strength to get through the day. Prayer needs to be constant, to be a source of continually talking to God, and needs to be given a useful, regular period of time to spend with Him, our creator.

Prayer does not have to be confined to your regular daily period. There are plenty of times for prayer and praise throughout the day as things happen to us. We may see a beautiful scenic view and want to praise God for it. We may find ourselves in a difficult situation and need God to strengthen us. We can shoot arrow prayers, one-liners, and they really work.

There may be a situation that you encounter in which you are not really involved, such as a road accident that you are just passing by. Pray for anyone who may be injured and for the emergency services. We are told to love our neighbours and to care for them. If we cannot physically do anything, we can still pray.

At work there are situations which may arise between two people not seeing eye-to-eye over how to do something. An argument may develop. Pray for them and the situation, and ask God if you should intervene and how. We need to be aware of what is happening around us and for people's needs for prayer.

I encountered a problem with two work colleagues who had a difference of opinion. I prayed for the situation and praised God that in twenty-four hours they were getting on again and the problem had passed. I was amazed how God had worked in that situation, as no human reasoning, rational arguments or lengthy talks with both persons could have brought that result so quickly.

God can and will work in any situation if we ask Him and have faith that He will work. Prayer is our channel. It is essential to stay tuned in and not to move off the waveband. Prayer is powerful! Prayer is life-changing! It is our lifeline. Prayer works!

# Chapter Seven

# Our Attitudes, Behaviour and Time Use

**John 15:19**
*If you belonged to the world, it would love you as its own. As it is you do not belong to the world, but I have chosen you out of the world. That is why the world hates you.*

What does it really mean to be *in* the world but not *part* of the world?

God has chosen us; isn't that fantastic?! God, the creator of the universe, the person who existed before anything else, has chosen us! We should act as people who respect this great fact and who want to do just what He wants. However, sadly, the behaviour of some Christians is far from what it ought to be. It would seem that they have a two-tiered idea of Christian behaviour: one outlook for Sundays and church events and another for the rest of the time.

When you see people in their own homes, their attitudes and behaviour patterns really show. It is one thing to keep up an outward façade to friends at church, but it is difficult to portray something that you are not when at home, when the barriers are down and we are vulnerable.

Many people fall into this habit of not really living as Jesus wants and told us to. I am not saying that we should all be 'goody-goodies', but rather that we should live out our lives as followers of Jesus and, in so doing, show others His love through our behaviour and attitudes.

**Romans 13:13,14**
*Let us behave decently, as in the daytime, not in orgies and drunkenness, not in sexual immorality and debauchery, not in dissension and jealousy. Rather, clothe yourselves with the Lord*

*Jesus Christ, and do not think about how to gratify the desires of the sinful nature.*

**Philippians 1:9-10**
*And this is my prayer: that your love may abound more and more in knowledge and depth of insight, so that you may be able to discern what is best and may be pure and blameless until the day of Christ.*

Over and over again in the Bible we are told to lead blameless lives[25], so why is it that so many of us don't? Why is it that we call ourselves Christians when we are not truly living up to that title?

We need to consider carefully what Paul said concerning the right way of living a Christian life when he wrote to the Ephesians. What he said is equally true for us today. Take the time to read Ephesians 4:17-5:20 (see Appendix for the full text).

Through our behaviour and our attitudes to a variety of things, people will see us for who we are. If we always follow the crowd and are swayed by the majority view then people may say, "They are Christians but they still get drunk, swear and tell smutty stories."

This is all too true today. If we really seek God's will as to where and what He wants us to be and do, then He will give us the strength to say no to the things that we know are not right for us. We are able to give the reasons for not doing something and make a stand for Christ. An opportunity may arise for you to share your faith with others, which is much better than doing those other things.

To stick out from the crowd is not wrong; it shows that you have the guts to be different. It does not matter if people think that you are odd or strange; it is what matters to God which is important. He is there with you in every situation. He is not going to let you fall into trouble.[26] If you obey His commands you have far more on your side than anyone else.

Our attitudes at work can also play an important part in our Christian living. There will often be friction between some work colleagues, and as a Christian you may be drawn into discussions, arguments or even teased or picked on by others. This is where the human element of speaking before you think, or doing something and ignoring the consequences, might easily happen. If you are in that situation, shoot an arrow prayer to God. He will help you with what

---

[25] See also Psalm 101:1-4; Proverbs 28:18
[26] See Psalm 55:22

to say and the correct things to do, which will often diffuse a fuming situation.

**Proverbs 3:1-6**
*My son, do not forget my teaching, but keep my commands in your heart, for they will prolong your life many years and bring you prosperity. Let love and faithfulness never leave you; bind them around your neck, write them on the tablet of your heart. Then you will win favour and a good name in the sight of God and man. Trust in the Lord with all your heart and lean not on your own understanding, in all your ways acknowledge Him and He will make your paths straight.*

When we think of doing something or going somewhere, whether it is with others or just on our own, we need to always consider whether God would want us to do that or to be there.

Remember, Jesus said that He is with us always. He is right next to us and His Spirit dwells in us all the time. We can hide nothing from Him; He sees and knows everything. When we dwell on this truth, it is even more important for us to get right with God in every situation, in every thought that we think and every word we say.

Even if we can sort out our outward behaviour, we still have to control one of the most problematical areas: our thoughts, which can spark off our behaviour and attitudes in a wrong direction. The only real way of doing this is to let God fully control our thoughts and bring us up sharp if we start to waiver. It is very easy under pressure to revert back to thinking malicious or unkind thoughts about others, and it is worse in a church community as it shows up what people are truly like.

We need to ask God to control our tongue as well as our mind. So often we speak without thinking and the damage is already done.

**James 3:5-10**
*Likewise the tongue is a small part of the body, but it makes great boasts. Consider what a great forest is set on fire by a small spark. The tongue also is a fire, a world of evil among the parts of the body. It corrupts the whole person, sets the whole course of his life on fire, and is itself set on fire by hell. All kinds of animals, birds and reptiles and creatures of the sea are being tamed and have been tamed by man, but no man can tame the tongue. It is a restless evil, full of deadly poison. With the tongue we praise our Lord and Father, and with it we curse men, who have been made in God's likeness. Out of the same mouth come praise and cursing. My brothers, this should not be.*

With God's joy in our hearts and His love enveloping us, we should be able to shine out for Him and to show His love to others through our behaviour and attitudes which are now in tune with His ways.

> 1 Peter 2:12-15
> *Live such good lives among the pagans that, though they accuse you of doing wrong, they may see your good deeds and glorify God on the day He visits us. Submit yourselves for the Lord's sake to every authority instituted among men ... For it is God's will that by doing good you should silence the ignorant talk of foolish men.*

Time waits for no man. The right use of time is important. Time is precious to us; we can become very possessive of the time we have in which to do something. In our busy lives, time to be alone is important, but if anyone or anything encroaches on that time we become resentful – to the point of making anyone who tries to speak to us during our time alone know that they have intruded on our time which we have put aside to do something special in.

This can so often happen at work. If there is an assignment to do and you have set an hour aside at the beginning of the day to do it, but the telephone keeps ringing and people come to ask questions, then by the end of that hour you can feel wretched. The consequences are that your work colleagues will give you a very wide berth so as not to incur your wrath. For the rest of that day you feel utterly useless.

This can easily happen at home and at church. We want time to do things that we want to do and have an agenda for each day of the week. We don't seem to understand that other people, even our own family, do not know about our agenda. Our answer to their question is, "Well, it's my time; I can do what I want. Why should I tell everyone what I am going to do each day?"

We tend to forget that all time is God's. He wants us to enjoy ourselves and have time to relax and be with our families and friends, but He also wants us to use our time in the best way possible. "Time waits for no one," I remember being told at school, when the usual excuse for not finishing study work was, "I ran out of time." The teacher said that I would have to make time. We know that only God can actually make time, but we can prayerfully consider each day and plan ahead with knowledge of what we have to do and what we would like to do if there is any time left over.

We have to get our priorities in order and make allowances if things take longer than expected. Good planning is essential, especially if we are leading busy lives. We need to give God our priority time and make sure that we schedule into our day a specific space to pray and read the Bible.

God has given us time for everything[27] if only we would stop and think and pray to Him, to help us through each day and week, to enable us use our time as He wants us to. It can be wasted so easily, and once it has gone there is nothing we can do to get it back. We need to look at what available time we have each week, after our working hours are over or before they start, to make room for what God would have us do.

We need to schedule time to be...

- with God
- with our family
- at church
- involved in Christian work (e.g. youth work, home groups)
- with friends
- alone

For those of us with a full time job, this will tend to dominate our time; however, we need to be very careful that we do not become workaholics and crowd out virtually everything else. We will become too tired and be of no use to anyone, even unable to get involved in church work. Of course we need to do our jobs properly and correctly and to spend time at work efficiently for our employer, but there comes a point when overtime gets to become extended time and then just the usual time, as you increase your normal hours at work to be there longer and longer.

The human body was made by God to fulfil certain functions and criteria, and I am sure that it was not made to be only a works machine!

There is a quality in most people of wanting to be acceptable to others. If we are asked to do something, we will say yes, if the task is not outrageous. This often leads to us taking on so many additional things that our time is again choked up, so that nothing we do is really done well.

[27] See Ecclesiastes 3:1-14; Psalm 31: 15

God wants us to do things well and to be effective, but we do have to say no sometimes. When we do, it should be in a manner of graciousness and not a sharp remark. It may well be that we could find a less busy person who is willing to do it. So often, especially in churches, it does appear that the majority of the work is done by a minority of the congregation. Ask God to guide you as to where He wants you to use your time within His Church.

It may be that He wants you to be a background person, encouraging others in their work by prayer and practical encouragement. If so, that is fine; the Church today really needs encouraging.

> **Romans 12:6-8**
> *We have different gifts according to the grace given us. If a man's gift is prophesying let him use it in proportion to his faith. If it is serving, let him serve, if it is teaching , let him teach, if it is encouraging , let him encourage, if it is contributing to the needs of others, let him give generously, if it is leadership, let him govern diligently, if it is showing mercy let him do it cheerfully.*

Our time is God's time. If we are carefully considering how we should use it God will open the opportunities up to us to serve Him, both in the Church and elsewhere.

We are by no means all called by God to be preachers and teachers, but we all have our part to play in God's world and especially within His Church.

> **1 Corinthians 12:27-28**
> *Now you are the body of Christ, and each one of you is a part of it. And in the church God has appointed first of all apostles, second prophets, third teachers, then workers of miracles, also those having gifts of healing, those able to help others, those with gifts of administration and those speaking in different kinds of tongues.*

God's people are multi-facetted, having all been given different qualities and gifts by God. We are each unique, and we all have something to give to His Church. Time is an enormous issue, because time is in the centre of how we exist. Everything we do is controlled by it. Clocks and watches, although telling us how much time we have left, do hinder our openness and our ability just to relax and dwell on God and to spend a proportion of His space with others.

We are always saying, "Oh, look at the time; I must be going!" or sometimes the preacher in church will look at the clock and say, "I'm sorry, I have gone on too long already, we must close now." God's work is stifled. We have a constant hang-up about what we must achieve in a certain twenty-four hour period.

It is better to plan ahead and consider those things that we need *not* really do for the sake of staying longer at a church meeting, or praying with others, or lending a listening ear to someone's problems.

A right use of time is essential for us as Christians, to allow God to use us as He wants. We have seen that we need to be effective for Christ and to become bold in what He has placed on our hearts to do, to enable us to make the transition from the complacent, existing and rutty Christian to one who knows God as a real person who is with them in everything – knowing His Spirit as a person who dwells within them and guides their thoughts and deeds as a person controlled one hundred per cent by God.

This Christian has the fervour to tell others about God and to get up from their easy chair and get stuck into the work that God had planned for them, to be a stick of dynamite for God, to spread the fire and power of God's word through their locality.

We have seen that once a person has acknowledged that what they are doing as a Christian is not entirely what God wants, and have understood how they should be living their Christian life, they can see the huge gap between the two lifestyles.

The Christian can build up their walk with God through...

- regular Bible reading.
- effective prayer
- correct behaviour and attitudes
- the right use of time

The Church needs dynamic Christians who are living for God and are thirsty for His Spirit to equip the Church, God's people, to change the world. We have to start with the change in our own lives, which will have the effect of God's love being shared out to all those around us.

# CHAPTER EIGHT

# The Armour of God

Another very important fact that we need to consider in the spiritual battles ahead is to know and use the whole armour of God. No soldier goes into war without a weapon and protection against the enemy. God also gives us protection and weapons so that we can be equipped and ready.

> **Ephesians 6:13**
> *Therefore put on the full armour of God, so that when the day of evil comes, you may be able to stand your ground, and after you have done everything, to stand.*

With an increase in our activity for God, the devil will increase his activity to disrupt us and put us off our course with God. He will sow doubts in our minds about what we are doing and whether it is right and from God. He will put attitudes into our minds saying, "Isn't it better to be as you were rather than to bother doing all these new things? Don't try too hard!" The devil is wily, clever and a master of undermining human qualities. He hates Christians; they upset his plans of evil!

We need to be alert and ready for these attacks; we need to stand firm and be strong. Our adversary is powerful, so we need God's greater power to help us.

> **Ephesians 6:12**
> *For our struggle is not against flesh and blood, but against authorities, against powers of this dark world and against the spiritual forces of evil in the heavenly realms.*

We are to fight the battle with God at our side, to realise that although we are in the body of Christ we each have our own personal battles to win, so that we can come together as a whole body of Christ and be a mighty force for God. God gives us His armour to wear so that we can go into battle knowing that what we are wearing has been proved as an effective defence and weapon against the enemy, since before our world existed.

## The belt of truth

> **Ephesians 6:14a**
> *Stand firm then with the belt of truth buckled round your waist.*

The belt is to be worn around our waist; it will hold the strength of God around us. God's truth will surround us and we will not be easily swayed from our firm position. Jesus was prophesied as having this same belt. It is with the knowledge of what Jesus has done for us and of how much He loves us that we can know His truth.

Truth must be uppermost in our Christian lives. To speak the truth in all our conversations is our first rule. Without truth we will fall into the devil's hands easily.

In certain situations to tell the truth might be very hard. It might be easier to slip in a half truth or to slightly alter the truth, to make it seem that your actions are acceptable when in fact you know that they are not. Truth has been referred to in the Bible many, many times. It is such an important element of God's plan for His people that without truth in the world we would have complete anarchy.

God is the founder of all truth, and if we are to follow in His plan and do as He says then it follows that we must be truthful in all our dealings, both large and small, at work and at home.

When Jesus was on the cross, dying, he cried out:

> **Luke 23:46a**
> *"Father into your hands I commit my spirit."*

This was a direct quote from Psalm 31:5, which continues:

> **Psalm 31:5b**
> *...Redeem me O Lord, the God of Truth.*

Both the Psalmist and Jesus recognised the importance of truth. Jesus was truthful throughout His life and especially in His trial before His death. He obeyed God and carried out His will, dying on the cross for us. He was true to the end. He didn't fail God.

We fail God regularly – but is it intentional? Do we calculate a situation and choose not to say the whole truth? Truth is sometimes very difficult to cope with, but from it comes reward. God wants us to be truthful and He will be with us in every moment of our anxiousness or nervousness. God won't let us down.

A belt is used to keep trousers or other garments up, around the waist. It gives us peace of mind and assuredness that when we step outside, our clothes won't end up around our ankles! Truth is like that; it is described as a belt because it won't let us down. It is an essential part of the spiritual armour, keeping it together and in place. Without the belt of truthfulness, the armour would fall down, which would lead to the soldier being injured. We all need to adhere to truth, for it is essential.

## The breastplate of righteousness

> **Ephesians 6:14b**
> *...with the breastplate of righteousness in place.*

A soldier in Bible times would have worn protection against arrows. The breastplate was important as it covered the chest and therefore protected the heart. This too will be our defence. God's breastplate will give us a defence and will also give us a character of being peace-loving, not promoting battles but ready if they come against us.

> **Isaiah 59:17**
> *He put on righteousness as His breastplate and the helmet of salvation on His head; He put on the garments of vengeance and wrapped himself in zeal as a cloak.*

We are putting on the same armour as the Lord.[28] It is a marvellous thing that Jesus gives us, His own armour to wear. To have a proper defence in any situation gives the ability to weigh up the prospect before us. Many times in the Christian life there will be spiritual battles in which we need a defence against the devil's arrows. He will do all he can to knock us off our road with Christ, to make us doubt our Christianity, to tempt us with things that we should avoid.

We need to be ready to defend our Christian life. To do this we can ground ourselves in the Bible, God's word, and in prayer. We need to be equipped by God to do His will. A good defence leads to the battle being won. Jesus wants us to lean on Him, and He will provide us with the power to withhold the things that come against

---

[28] See also Isaiah 11:5

us. We are to stand firm and protect ourselves, with God's help, in the life that we are leading. We are to be focused on Christ at all times, knowing that we have a King who has won the victory over the devil and that we are part of His family. We are to wear the breastplate boldly and be ready to do God's will as we go out with Him into the work that He has called us to do.

## The gospel of peace

> **Ephesians 6:15**
> *With your feet fitted with the readiness that comes from the gospel of peace.*

The gospel of peace is to be fitted as shoes onto our feet so that we are ready to go into battle and know that our feet are protected, just as the Roman soldiers' feet were, by means of supportive shoes. It enables us to be ready for what lies ahead and leads us to act in a peaceful manner, not forcing people into following Jesus but gently explaining how much Jesus loves and cares about them and how much He wants them to be assured of eternal life. We can let people see God's peace flowing from us, and we are ready to listen to His commands.

To be peaceful in our dealings with others is another essential element of being a Christian. We are called to be Christ-like and in so doing to demonstrate to those around us that to be a follower of Jesus is not to be an aggressive Bible-basher but rather a caring, comforting person who is interested in the needs of others.

In the Sermon on the Mount, Jesus taught us that peacemakers are blessed and will be called sons of God.[29] Peaceful people who strive to bring peace into the world are to be held in high esteem as they do their work for God, whether in a private and personal way or those on the world's political scene.

Peace is the essence to bring a society to a position where it is able to be ready to hear what God wants to say to it. People today are so busy that they have no time for God. They are looking after themselves. If we are truthful, then out of that frame of mind and way of living will come peace. If we are in tune with God there is no need to be agitated with ourselves or with others. God is in control of all affairs. We need to trust in Him.

---

[29] See Matthew 5:9

When Jesus is talking to His disciples about His death, He tells them that God will send the Holy Spirit to be with them. He then goes on to say:

**John 14:27**
*Peace I leave with you. My peace I give you. I do not give to you as the world gives. Do not let your hearts be troubled and do not be afraid.*

Later Jesus again tells His disciples that it will not be any easy ride being a Christian in the world. His statement below is one to cling to.

**John 16:33**
*I have told you these things so that in me you may have peace. In this world you will have trouble. But take heart I have overcome the world.*

Jesus says this only a few days before His death, at a time when we would expect sorrow and anguish. Jesus does not lead His followers into despair; rather he states His victory through His death, the ultimate end to God's rescue plan for mankind. Jesus can boldly state that He has overcome the world. No one else *could* ever, *can* ever or *will* ever say that again. Jesus is the eternal peacemaker.

## The shield of faith

**Ephesians 6:16**
*In addition to all this, take up the shield of faith, with which you can extinguish all the flaming arrows of the evil one.*

Shields were used to fend off both men and, more importantly, the waves of arrows which fell from the skies like rain. In Roman days the shields were covered in leather and soaked in water, to extinguish the flame-tipped arrows sent by the enemy.

With the shield of faith we can fend off the devil's arrows sent to wound us and stop us moving forward in our Christian life, resulting in thoughts of "What am I doing here?" easily entering our minds.

In our Christian lives it is vital to have faith in Jesus. Faith is that essential component that allows us to acknowledge Jesus as a reality. Without faith the Christian life would be meaningless. God looks after us in all things, which we can know through our faith in Him. We are shielded by God's awesome power, kept from danger by our relationship with Him.

In Peter's first letter to the Christians who had been scattered throughout the world, he greeted them and underlined that their living hope is Jesus. He refers to suffering grief in all kinds of trials but that we have His shield around us.

> **1 Peter 1:5-6**
> *Who through faith are shielded by God's power until the coming of the salvation that is ready to be revealed in the last time. In this you greatly rejoice, though now for a little while you may have to suffer grief in all kinds of trials.*

This is exactly why we need to put on the whole spiritual armour of God.

## The helmet of salvation

> **Ephesians 6:17**
> *Take the helmet of salvation and the sword of the Spirit, which is the word of God.*

This provides us with protection and also gives us a sure knowledge of victory. We know that Jesus died for us and we have accepted Him into our lives as King. We are assured of salvation and therefore we know that God will win through. With that knowledge we know we will win the battle eventually, despite maybe going through a conflict.

The helmet for the soldier was a striking symbol of military victory. To see many helmets shining and upright coming towards you was worrying, to say the least, if your side only had loose garments and a quiver of arrows!

As with the breastplate of righteousness, God gives us *His* helmet which He wore to symbolise our salvation. Salvation is the culmination of our Christian lives. We have assurance that our sins are forgiven by God, through the death and resurrection of Jesus. Like a helmet protecting the soldier's head, God protects us by encompassing us with His love and power. We are weak but God is strong. The head is weak but the helmet is strong.

The knowledge of salvation gives us the ability to step out in faith, trusting God to be with us always. Salvation is not something that is ours by right. It is given us by God.

> **Revelation 7:10**
> *Salvation belongs to our God, who sits on throne, and to the Lamb.*

God and Jesus own our salvation; without them we have nothing. If we can understand this then we must understand that without faith in God we are nothing. We don't deserve to be saved from our sins but God is loving and merciful and will save us through His freely given grace if we say sorry and ask Him to forgive us. Although salvation protects us, it is not without a part for us to play.

> **Philippians 2:12-13**
> *Therefore my dear friends, as you have always obeyed, not only in my presence, but now much more in my absence, continue to work out your salvation with fear and trembling, for it is God who works in you to will and to act according to His good purpose.*

We can't stop what God wants just because we have salvation. Obedience is key to the Christian life and should come as a result of what God has done for us. A soldier's helmet was unique to that man. There may have been hundreds of the same-looking helmet in the battalions and legions in Roman times, but each helmet was made to fit the individual soldier's head. This was essential to make sure it fitted properly and would not fall off in battle or rub a sore area.

Salvation is also unique; no one else can give us the protection that God can give.[30] It is His gift to us – His unique rescue plan for His people.

## The sword of the Spirit

> **Ephesians 6:17**
> *Take the helmet of salvation and the sword of the spirit, which is the word of God.*

The sword is the soldier's weapon. If he went into battle and either did not take his sword or took it but didn't use it, he would not have been a very effective soldier and would not have lasted very long on the battlefield. Likewise, we in the spiritual battle will not last long if we don't have the word of God (the Bible) with us and in constant use. That is why it is so important to read the Bible regularly and to take in what God is saying to us.

God has not given us His word for nothing; we are meant to use it. It is the Christian's instruction manual. If we take time to read it, we will not only begin to understand what God is saying to us but also be able to make good use of it.

We have already noted the importance of setting aside time to study the Bible. Trying to live as a Christian without referring to the

---

[30] See Acts 4:12

Bible just won't work. We need to immerse ourselves in God's word, to see what He wants us to do on a daily basis. The soldier would have made sure that his sword was clean and sharp before going to battle so that he could rely on it to do the job it was made for. Likewise we need to keep our Bibles at the ready, not on the top shelf gathering dust!

The sword was the difference between *killing* the enemy and *being killed* by the enemy. The Bible is God's weapon against the devil's evil ways. We need to read, digest and act upon what we read in the Bible to enable us to fight the good fight for God.

## Pray in the Spirit.

> **Ephesians 6:19**
> *And pray in the Spirit on all occasions with all kinds of prayer and bequests. With this in mind, be alert and always keep on praying for all the saints.*

God speaks to us through prayer as well as His word, therefore we must pray to God on all occasions. Prayer, as we have seen earlier, is an essential part of our walk with God.

A soldier today keeps in touch with his headquarters by a radio operator in his platoon. The captain can be updated on enemy action and can call for help if he and his battalion are being pinned down by enemy fire. Prayer is rather like that; we can pray all kinds of prayers to God, and we need not always have the same format, as God will still listen to us. He will know what we need in the situation. It may be reassurance, guidance, strength to persevere or any number of other things. God will answer our prayers in the way and in the timing that He knows is best for us, which may not always be what we expect. We can be assured that God knows best in all things, and if we are allowing Him to be in control of our lives, then we need to learn to accept that what God says and does is best for us.

Apart from requests in prayer, we may wish just to pray for others who we know are in a spiritual battle, such as those in another country where it is more difficult to be a Christian and where physical persecution is a real danger. Always pray earnestly and really mean what you say. If we pray in a right spirit, we will find that answers to prayer come more frequently.

Prayer is a vital communication for the Christian. Regular prayer, both personal and with other Christians, will build up spiritual awareness and allow us to be in tune with what God wants. We are told to be alert in our prayers just as the soldier had to be alert at all times, ready to defend his position or to advance stealthily. We need to be alert and on the lookout for spiritual dangers, not only for ourselves but for our fellow Christians.

We are all part of the body of Christ; therefore we should be caring for each other in mind, body and spirit. In prayer God may say something to us which directly affects another's life. We may be prompted to visit someone in need or to pray for certain situations. By keeping alert and listening to God, we will discover a new plane for our relationship with Him.

We have better weapons in our armoury than the soldier of old, for we have God's weapons, those of divine power.

> 2 Corinthians 10:3-4
> *For though we live in the world, we do not wage war as the world does. The weapons we fight with are not the weapons of the world. On the contrary, they have divine power to demolish strongholds.*

Put on the whole armour of God and live your life as God intended, immersed in Him and with a personal relationship with Jesus.

# Chapter Nine

## What Are You Going to Do Now?

It will soon be time for you to decide how you are going to move forward in your life. What is the next step for you to take? Let's review what we have learned, pulling all the angles together so that you can see the whole picture, consider where you stand with God and ponder on where He wants you to be and what He wants you to be doing. We will do this with the aid and experience of a guy called Dave.

Dave didn't really have any real spiritual backbone, but he thought his life was not too bad. His Christian life was one where Sundays meant going twice to church with his friends – a place where he took part in worship, but somehow it didn't really mean very much to him.

On Monday, Dave was very much the same as anyone else at work; he enjoyed joining in with everyone else in the evening, whatever they were doing. It didn't really matter, and it would have been a pity to spoil things by not going just because he was a Christian!

Dave had little self-control and he followed his own will in most things, which unfortunately was crowding out God's will and pushing God into a box. Dave only released God from the box when he was in trouble or despair – and of course when he went to church on Sundays. However, Dave usually knew what to do on Sundays because it was all routine!

Dave knew about the love of God and all the facts about why He had sent Jesus into the world – but that was as far as it went. God was out there somewhere looking down on him, and he was down on earth looking up at Him. God wasn't accessible. He was far off. Dave could not grasp the concept of being a child before his heavenly

Father and really *knowing* God and having His presence engulf and surround him.

He was in his own rut and was content to stay there, being blinkered to what God wanted to do for Him and what God had planned for his life. Dave's faith was no more than an intellectual knowledge stating that, "There is a God. He made heaven and earth. He came to earth at Christmas, did some amazing miracles, died on the cross at Easter and rose from the dead." Faith was not a meaningful experience of the glory of God. There was no ability or even longing to know more about God; Dave was content to live as he was, without encountering a real faith.

God, Jesus and the Holy Spirit were all known of by Dave, but beyond knowing *about* them there was no real sense of a personal relationship with the most important people in the universe. He was not really able to comprehend the amount of love that God had for him, nor able to understand the power which all Christians have with access to the Holy Spirit.

The bottom line was that Dave didn't want to completely let go of all the pre-conceived and pre-understood ideas and concepts that he had about being a Christian. He was unable to see beyond his own human horizon to God's glorious new horizon.

Dave was not letting God have complete control of every corner of his life. He wanted to hold on to those very private areas. He was opening the door and saying to Jesus, "Come in and dwell in me, but just sit over there and be quiet. Don't rock the boat! I will call you when I need you."

The Christian life is not supposed to be like this. As Christians, we have been given so much by God – so why do we buttonhole God as just another possession to be used, as and when we please?

There are so many people today just like Dave, who are really only scratching the surface of being a Christian. If our world is going to be changed and challenged by the Gospel of Christ, then Christians, as the body of Christ, need to be totally effective.

It's no good saying, "Yes, I understand the problem, but get someone else to do it." We all have a responsibility to play our part for God. It is this realisation of the need in our world and the power of the word of God which the Christian should put together and conclude that God is the only answer for the world.

That is why God sent Jesus, our Saviour, to die for our sins – to enable the world to come back to Him. He is the world's rescuer and

Saviour; no one else can get this world of men and women back into a personal relationship with God, their creator. We need to act for God in His world.

How are we to act so that we achieve this goal?

**Matthew 28:18-20**
*Then Jesus came to them and said, "All authority in heaven and on earth has been given to me. Therefore go and make disciples of all nations, baptising them in the name of the Holy Spirit, and teaching them to obey everything I have commanded you. And surely I am with you always, to the very end of the age."*

Jesus gave us the command, He pulled the trigger of the starting gun and started the race, but where are we on the track? Have we fallen at the first hurdle? The Christian race is not a smooth dash to the finish; it is an obstacle course with many pitfalls and hazards along the way.

The more we get into the race, the more obstacles appear, being put in by Satan, who wants us to retire injured. God has given us so much and has shown us in the Bible how to live as Christians and how to be effective for Him. He will guide us through the obstacles, if we keep our eyes firmly fixed on Him.

**Hebrews 12:1-2**
*Therefore, since we are surrounded by such a great cloud of witnesses, let us throw off everything that hinders and the sin that so easily entangles, and let us run with perseverance, the race marked out for us. Let us fix our eyes on Jesus, the author and perfecter of our faith, who for the joy set before Him endured the cross, succumbing its shame and sat down at the right hand of the throne of God.*

God will hold us and give us the strength needed to get to the finishing line. As the Christian comes into realisation of God's power and the might of His glorious Son who died for us, and of His Holy Spirit who dwells within us and gives us the power of Jesus to enable us to do so much for God, he can do nothing else but to ask God to fully control his life and to come in and cleanse him from all the wrong things that have been there, including the wrong attitudes about God and the Christian life.

It is time to start afresh, to go back to the blocks, tighten the shoes and fix our gaze on the starter of all things, God our creator. This time there will be no false starts. This time we need to have the right emphasis, the right outlook. Our starter is going to run the race as well. He will be our guide. Jesus is always with us. He is our friend with whom we can relate. He is a real person who wants to be talked to, just as we converse with our friends.

Jesus wants to be part of our inner circle of close friends. In fact, He wants to be our closest friend. He has every right to be so after what He has done for us. We have to be vigilant in our walk with God. We must not let others try and talk us out of what we have in Christ.

If we are to live wholeheartedly for God and have Him in total control of our lives, we have to make a decision: do we really intend to live this out? If you have decided to say yes to go forward now with Jesus in full control of your life, then you must stick to it, whatever comes your way. Don't let those human doubts crowd into your mind. Remember how Peter walked on the water when Jesus called him?[31] Peter had faith that if he fixed his eyes on Jesus, he also could walk to Him on the water.

> **Matthew 14:30**
> *But when he saw the wind, he was afraid and, beginning to sink, cried out, "Lord save me."*

Peter suddenly realised where he was and looked away from Jesus. Fear crowded in and his faith started to fall away. Peter knew who Jesus was and what He could do but his own thoughts and fears took over.

We will have times in our walk with God when doubts will come into our minds, and we will listen to people around us saying that this new experience of Jesus won't last for long, it will be over soon and we will be back to normal. Sadly many Christians, including some Christian leaders, do not fully understand the concept of the real love, presence and power of God. They know the theology behind it and they are able to talk about it, but they are not experiencing it in their own lives. Unfortunately, if they are not one hundred per cent in tune with God they will invariably cast doubt upon the beliefs and behaviour of those Christians who are experiencing His daily presence and power.

If we were not meant to live a life wholly devoted to God and His divine majesty, and be able to have use of His power, then God would not have said through Jesus that Christians would receive power when the Holy Spirit comes upon them. He also added, "And

---

[31] Matthew 14:22-36

you will be my witnesses in Jerusalem, and in all Judea and Samaria and to the ends of the earth." (Acts 1:8)

Although Jesus was then speaking to the early church leaders, it was not just for them; otherwise God would not have recorded it in His inspired word. We are to reach the whole world, not just parts of the world. The Bible is to be read in its entirety as it is our instruction book. Who are we to pick and choose what we read of God's word, leaving out those parts which may cause us to have to change our views?

The words of Jesus, both commands and advice to those early church leaders, are just as important for us today, for we are facing many of the same problems in our world as they were then.

If we come to know God totally, as we have been discovering, we will have an inner strength. Our very being will be transformed to do the will of Christ, and through us God can do His mighty works on His earth.

> **2 Peter 1:3**
> *His divine power has given us everything we need for life and godliness through our knowledge of Him who called us by His own glory and goodness.*

When we are living a truly faithful life for Christ, we have the sure knowledge that what we have is right and from God. It will give us excitement to see what God will do through us and for his people. If people question our faith or our 'new' behaviour, it is an opportunity to share what has happened in our lives, telling them about our new realisation and awareness of Christ, the refreshed knowledge of God's love.[32] We are to become God's ambassadors on His earth, to show His love to others through what we do and say.

As God loves us so much, we are to reflect that love and to serve Him in our lives. We are to be beacons for Him in our communities.

> **Acts 3:19-20**
> *Repent, then, and turn to God, so that your sins may be wiped out, that times of refreshing may come from the Lord, and that He may send the Christ, who has been appointed for you – even Jesus.*

We all need a time to rest when we can recharge our batteries. This is also true in the spiritual battle; we need to continuously ask

---

[32] See Ephesians 3:16-19

God to fill us with His power, to continue His work. When Jesus spoke through the miracles, things happened. It was God's hand which transformed Jesus' words into actions. God's hand will be, and is, in all we do for Him. He will enable us to talk lovingly to those who question us about why we have got up out of the rut of ordinary, respectable Christianity, with all the manmade trimmings that go with it, and moved into a new and eager spirituality, into a life that is refreshed and ready to do God's work. We will have joy in our hearts which will be seen in our lives.

We need to be bold so that we can speak the word of God in its entirety and its truth, so that others will also want to be transformed into effective Christians. I implore you, therefore, not to keep God in a box for emergency use only but to declare His marvellous majesty, power and might and to acknowledge that He is the only true God and the one whom you want to serve, one hundred per cent, and whom you will let control your whole life.

There is nothing better than to know the real and glorious presence of God engulfing your very being, and the realisation of His love and truth in your life. So, I urge you to be firmly grounded in God the rock,[33] ready with His armour around you to do whatever He has planned for you, and to have a true and lasting faith. What God says, happens. Will you obey Him and do what He has told you to do? No more fence sitting, it's doing time!

I have found such an enormous difference in my life since I said, "Yes, God, I will let you have total control, and I will do what you want me to do, knowing that you are with me, giving me your strength and power to deal with each situation as it comes along."

If you have found God talking to you as you have read this book, challenging you to change your attitude towards your life and towards Him, then I encourage you to do something about it. Become an effective, dynamic Christian as God intended you to be.

In Acts 10, Peter was not happy about going to the Gentiles, but he obeyed God and recognised that what God had told Him to do was going to make a huge impact in the world and was part of God's plan.[34] The narrative explains that the reason Peter was sent for was that Cornelius and his family wanted to hear about Jesus and to be

---

[33] See Psalm 18:2
[34] See Acts 10:28-29

baptised. God had a plan for Peter that was out of his comfort zone, but he responded obediently, and as a result God used him mightily.

Are you going to respond obediently to God? Let God out of the box, to be free to work in your life and through you, in the lives of others. If we are open and willing to listen to what God is saying to us, then we are in a right frame of mind to receive what God wants and to be enabled to be an effective tool for Christ.

I invite you to use the following prayer as you start out on a new path with your God. If you have not yet truly acknowledged God as your Saviour, then join with me and open your heart to Him now and invite Him in, to dwell with you and give you the certainty of eternal life.

> *Dear Lord and Saviour,*
>
> *I come before you and acknowledge that I have not been living my life as you have intended. I am deeply sorry and seek your forgiveness for all the things that I have done in my life that have not been according to your plan. Thank you for dying for me and taking away my sins and giving me another chance to have a fresh start with you.*
>
> *Lord, I open my heart and ask that you would come and dwell in me, to the full. I realise that I need you to fill me totally and that without you I am nothing. I know that you are alive today and are with me. Help me to be strong and bold for you as I encounter all that life has for me, and enable me to be a true ambassador for you.*
>
> *Amen.*

I would recommend that you tell someone about your new experience and share with them what God has done for you.

What a difference we would see in our nation and in the world if all believers would obey God's word and live as true followers of Christ, putting Him first and self last. Through living as Christ wants us to, we will experience a new joy and peace which only He can give us.

Don't delay! Open the box and let God out! Surrender totally to Him. You won't regret it. Do it now!

# Appendix

# One Hundred Per Cent for God

Ephesians 4:17-5:20

*So I tell you this, and insist on it in the Lord, that you must no longer live as the Gentiles do, in the futility of their thinking. They are darkened in their understanding and separated from the life of God because of the ignorance that is in them due to the hardening of their hearts. Having lost all sensitivity, they have given themselves over to sensuality so as to indulge in every kind of impurity, and they are full of greed.*

*That, however, is not the way of life you learned when you heard about Christ and were taught in him in accordance with the truth that is in Jesus. You were taught, with regard to your former way of life, to put off your old self, which is being corrupted by its deceitful desires; to be made new in the attitude of your minds; and to put on the new self, created to be like God in true righteousness and holiness.*

*Therefore each of you must put off falsehood and speak truthfully to your neighbor, for we are all members of one body. "In your anger do not sin": Do not let the sun go down while you are still angry, and do not give the devil a foothold. Anyone who has been stealing must steal no longer, but must work, doing something useful with their own hands, that they may have something to share with those in need.*

*Do not let any unwholesome talk come out of your mouths, but only what is helpful for building others up according to their needs, that it may benefit those who listen. And do not grieve the Holy Spirit of God, with whom you were sealed for the day of redemption. Get rid of all bitterness, rage and anger, brawling and slander, along with every form of malice. Be kind and compassionate to one another, forgiving each other, just as in Christ God forgave you. Follow God's example, therefore, as dearly loved children and walk in the way of love, just as Christ loved us and gave himself up for us as a fragrant offering and sacrifice to God.*

*But among you there must not be even a hint of sexual immorality, or of any kind of impurity, or of greed, because these are improper for God's holy people. Nor should there be obscenity, foolish talk or coarse joking, which are out of place, but rather thanksgiving. For of this you can be sure: No immoral, impure or greedy person—such a person is an idolater—has any inheritance in the kingdom of Christ and of God. Let no one deceive you with empty words, for because of such things God's wrath comes on those who are disobedient. Therefore do not be partners with them.*

*For you were once darkness, but now you are light in the Lord. Live as children of light (for the fruit of the light consists in all goodness, righteousness and truth) and find out what pleases the Lord. Have nothing to do with the fruitless deeds of darkness, but rather expose them. It is shameful even to mention what the disobedient do in secret. But everything exposed by the light becomes visible—and everything that is illuminated becomes a light. This is why it is said:*

> *"Wake up, sleeper,*
> *rise from the dead,*
> *and Christ will shine on you."*

*Be very careful, then, how you live—not as unwise but as wise, making the most of every opportunity, because the days are evil. Therefore do not be foolish, but understand what the Lord's will is. Do not get drunk on wine, which leads to debauchery. Instead, be filled with the Spirit, speaking to one another with psalms, hymns, and songs from the Spirit. Sing and make music from your heart to the Lord, always giving thanks to God the Father for everything, in the name of our Lord Jesus Christ.*

# Related Books by the Publisher

**Out of the Pigpen**
Jo Wright
ISBN: 978-1-907509-70-4

Jo Wright encourages us to live day by day in the fulness of God's plan for our lives. How do we deal with the gap between what we believe on Sunday and what we experience through the rest of the week? Just as the Prodigal Son in Jesus' parable recognized that his life in the pigpen was far from his Father's best, so we too can choose to walk 'out of the pigpen' and into our spiritual inheritance.

**The Language of Knowing Our Heavenly Father's Heart and Will**
Leon Gosiewski
ISBN: 978-1-907509-59-9

The author unpacks what the scriptures have to say about knowing our heavenly Father, Jesus and the Holy Spirit on a relational level. Common misconceptions and unhelpful teachings are highlighted, and there is a call to return to a walk of holiness in which God is truly honoured as Lord and Saviour.

**Redeeming a Nation**
Philip Quenby
ISBN: 978-1-907509-40-7

Philip Quenby has produced a most unique and timely book of English historical episodes and characters from a Christian perspective. It presents a fascinating perspective of God's intervention in the affairs of a great nation – England. More than ever before, there is a need for this generation to find its moral and cultural bearings, in order to navigate towards social wisdom and stability.